THE SELF CONSCIOUS
IMAGINATION

UNIVERSITY OF
NEWCASTLE UPON TYNE
PUBLICATIONS

THE
SELF CONSCIOUS
IMAGINATION

A Study of
the Coleridge notebooks in
celebration of the bi-centenary of
his birth 21 October 1772

The Riddell Memorial Lectures
Forty-fourth Series
delivered at the
University of Newcastle upon Tyne
on 20, 21, 22 February 1973

BY

KATHLEEN COBURN

Professor Emeritus of English,
Victoria College in the University of Toronto

LONDON
OXFORD UNIVERSITY PRESS
NEW YORK   TORONTO
1974

Oxford University Press, Ely House, London W.1

GLASGOW   NEW YORK   TORONTO   MELBOURNE   WELLINGTON
CAPE TOWN   SALISBURY   IBADAN   NAIROBI   LUSAKA   ADDIS ABABA
BOMBAY   CALCUTTA   MADRAS   KARACHI   LAHORE   DACCA
KUALA LUMPUR   HONG KONG

ISBN 0 19 713913 2

© *University of Newcastle upon Tyne 1974*

PRINTED IN GREAT BRITAIN
BY W & J MACKAY LIMITED
CHATHAM

A philosophy is an abstraction from an autobiography.

Sir Russell Brain *The Nature of Experience,*
The Riddell Memorial Lectures, 1958

PREFACE

THE Trustees of the Riddell Memorial Lectures invited me to deliver this series of lectures on the occasion of the bi-centenary of the birth of Samuel Taylor Coleridge. I gratefully accepted the honour they did me as an opportunity to share the pleasures of editing Coleridge's notebooks and of struggling to understand some of the processes of thought of an astonishing, influential, and still contemporary mind.

Toronto   K.C.

1973

CONTENTS

AUTHOR'S NOTE

In quoting from the notebooks I have taken a few small liberties with punctuation, cancellations, minor slips of the pen, and so on, in the interest of readability, but in the main the informal character and appearance of these private memoranda are maintained. Entries already published in my edition, *The Notebooks of Samuel Taylor Coleridge*, Bollingen Foundation, New York and Routledge & Kegan Paul, London (Vol. I, 1957, Vol. II, 1962, Vol. III, 1973) are referred to by volume and series number, under the abbreviation *CN*. Unpublished entries are referred to the MS notebook where they appear. Unless otherwise specified, any other works of Coleridge are quoted from the edition of *The Collected Works of S. T. Coleridge* now in progress, being published in England by Routledge & Kegan Paul and in the U.S. by Princeton University Press for Bollingen Foundation.

I

THE SELF-CONSCIOUS SELF

IN entitling these lectures 'The Self Conscious Imagination: a study of the Coleridge Notebooks' I have been guilty of a little Coleridgian word-play. The *Oxford English Dictionary* gives as the first meaning of *self-conscious*, 'Having consciousness of one's identity, one's actions, sensations, etc.; reflectively aware of one's actions'.[1] As the second definition of *self-conscious*, it gives the use more common today: 'Marked by undue or morbid pre-occupation with one's own personality; so far self-centred as to suppose one is the object of observation by others.' In this latter sense we apply it to the blushing, awkward person stricken by an exaggerated sense of being always somehow the prisoner at the bar, in fact so unable to be truly conscious of his own identity or actions as not to be in control of his own sensations, and so fumbling in the presence of judge and jury as to make himself appear to be the liar or the thief he imagines he is accused of being. The two senses of the word are thus antithetical, *self-conscious* (1) as being realistically accurate about one's identity, and *self-conscious* (2) as being anything but clear, in fact painfully in doubt. Now in both senses the phrase 'self-conscious imagination' is applicable to Coleridge. A study of his notebooks demonstrates that all his life he wrestled to conquer the

[1] And incidentally it refers to Coleridge and *Biographia Literaria* for the first use *in this sense* of the adjective—though the noun *self-consciousness* goes back earlier, to Locke.

applicability of the second meaning to himself, and to achieve the victory represented by the first, i.e., to make the transition from the fear and trembling of self-doubt and incompleteness, from all those dreadful excuses and apologies of the letters, to emotional freedom, steadiness, and wholeness of vision. In this respect he stands in anti-thesis, e.g., to Samuel Beckett, or at least to the non-heroes of Beckett's stories, whose search appears to be not for more, but for less and less self-consciousness—for inarticulateness and oblivion.

I intend to refer specifically and almost exclusively to the notebooks. Not that other fields are not tempting, but here we have a unique opportunity to watch him as in private he puts the injunction he and Socrates often quoted, 'Know Thyself', into practice. Critics have expounded, discussed, argued about, praised, and de-bunked Coleridge's poetry, philosophy, aesthetics, theology, scientific hypotheses, educational theories, economics, and have attributed them to the Germans, mental derangement, Plato, Jacobinical socialism, Wordsworth, mysticism, emotional immaturity, innate Toryism, and the eye and Betty Martin. But as we gather momentum now in producing Coleridge's *Collected Works* it becomes apparent that there is a little-known Coleridge who insisted on beginning at square one. It is never safe to disbelieve or dismiss him out of hand, or to fail to credit him with having investigated what he says he knows. The more one works on the texts the more fully one becomes aware of his insistence on questioning himself, and seeing for himself. This is the Coleridge of the notebooks.

Here is Coleridge in his most private, personal, unguarded, unhistrionic utterance. He is meditating on his experiences in the very act of experiencing. This is not Coleridge the poet, critic, reader, though he is always all of these. We shall not attempt to study Coleridge's intellectual development *per se*, nor survey his thought systematically (as distinct from his thoughts) nor defend his position. All these have been done, though not for all time—and sometimes brilliantly. What I should like mainly to do is to catch one of the great minds in human history in its wide ranges of introspection, observation, and analysis, looking at what interests him, and following his eye where his attention and imagination direct *him*—not us; we *are* peeping Toms.

The clearest way to make plain what is going on in Coleridge's notebooks will be to quote as many memoranda as possible. This I mean to do, for no one can convey Coleridge as well as he does himself. Yet perhaps a short general account may help one to visualize the notebooks.

There are about seventy of them, and I am not being guilefully vague about the exact number—or perhaps I am, for among the many uncertainties with which Coleridge immediately confronts an editor is the question, what is a notebook? Coleridge's are of various shapes, and range in size downwards from what he called 'the Folio Book' to small scraps of paper folded and stitched with what may have been Mrs. Gillman's crotchet cotton, in stitching that looks for all the world as if it may have been his own. He began to write in memorandum books in 1794—when he was twenty-two —at least we know of none earlier—and continued to do so until a few weeks before his death in July 1834 at the

age of sixty-two. In other words they cover a span of
forty years. He often had more than one notebook in
use—sometimes writing in one in the morning and
another in the evening of the same day for no discernible
systematic reason—and conversely notebooks were
apparently carelessly abandoned in pockets and desk
drawers and travelling cases, to be resurrected years
later and casually used again. Long periods could thus
intervene between one entry and the next. 'Twenty-
three years between the entries on this page!!!' he
noticed. He had a way of working from both ends of a
notebook, so that in at least one important case it is
difficult to tell which is front and which is back. In
another, N 3½, he had a momentary wild hope of keep-
ing a systematic German vocabulary book when he was
first learning the language. He divided the book into
sections according to subjects: 'Part the First, Names of
Spirits, Men, Birds, Beasts, Fishes, and Reptiles, and of
the constituent Parts of the Same.' Under this heading
there is a list of some seventeen German words and such
English equivalents as (to select but a few): 'Night-
Mairs, A barrow of garbage, a hobgoblin, the bend of
the knee, Crow-Carrion—the fly-blown Carcase, the
Reins, Night Ghosts, Nightingale, Peacock, Forehead, a
pair of swallows' wings, vermin, a water-toad.' Not, one
would think an approach to basic German. 'Part the
Second' dealt with the vocabulary of 'Sensation,
Passion, Touch, Taste, and Smell', the shorter list there
being made up of words like: 'Amazedness, Gouty or
paralytic, social, to foster P & M (physically & men-
tally)', and so on. Ten parts were thought of, but he
must soon have understood why dictionaries are usually

arranged alphabetically, for he soon lost himself, quickly deserted his scheme, and used N 3½ for the usual helter-skelter assortment.

There is a certain lightness of heart about his note-taking, as indeed there is frequently a charming lack of solemnity about him in general. Some of the notebooks he nicknamed 'Fly catchers', numbering them, and struggling to keep track of them as he grew older, reminding himself, e.g. in No. VIII that the beginning of such and such a discussion was in No. VI. There were other names for these little books too; in March 1827 he wrote in the first leaf of what we now know as Notebook 56: 'Volatilia or Day-Book for bird-liming Small Thoughts, impounding Stray Thoughts, and holding for trial doubtful Thoughts'. No one can accuse Coleridge of pomposity.

He set forth perfectly the state of his notebooks (and incidentally his own sense of humour in regard to them) in the front of Notebook 28:

16 July 1819   Highgate
(continued from the red-pocket book marked χημικο—φιλοσοφικον on the outside Cover)
That book like most of its Predecessors begins at beginning, middle and end—and to prevent the Jumble of Heterogene subjects resulting from this ταραξια κ'αταξια I have paged the last 28 (recommencing p. 1 after p. 160) sides separately, the side next the Cover being p. 28: and devote these exclusively to Miscellanea. [N 28 *f2*]

If these instructions convey confusion I can assure you, relatively speaking, what they convey is order itself. Coleridge had a *sense* of order, but he could not organize —neither could his daughter, Sara, nor his grandson

E.H.C., to judge by their transcripts of S.T.C.'s[1] MSS,
which are chaos compounded at a very high rate. In
spite of the chronological disorder, or rather the total
absence of a time order, the only way to present the
notebooks was chronological; without an attempt at a
rough chronological sequence much would be even
more mysterious than it intrinsically is.

We cannot too often remember that Coleridge's notebooks were never intended for the sight of another pair
of eyes. They are 'the history of my own mind for my
own improvement' he said [*CN* II 2368]; they were the
private reflections of a very sociable, very lonely man.
Sometimes he wrote in cipher—not that there was anything dreadful to conceal—because he felt, until at the
age of forty-four he reached the Gillmans in Highgate,
that he lived in a world in which at some point or other,
everyone—or was it he?—was a stranger.

One has only to look at the notebooks of some other
writers to see a special kind of solitariness in this con-
vivial, talkative person. These are and are not a writer's
notebooks; that is to say, Coleridge would have written
most of his seven thousand notebook entries had he not
been a writer. They are not directed towards his writing
—or only lightly and occasionally so. His notebooks are
what he called them, his 'dear Companions'. Compare
this with what some other writers have said.

Somerset Maugham tells us he did not make a single
note he did not intend to use in his writings. Leonardo,

---

[1] Their devotion to S.T.C.'s work was absolute, and we must all be
grateful to them for their diligence. They occasionally provide information we need, but in order to get it from their masses and messes of
papers we must thread labyrinths.

Matthew Arnold, Samuel Butler, Albert Camus, Dylan Thomas—a random list—all kept such work books. The notebooks of Gerard Manley Hopkins might seem a likely parallel, with Hopkins's interest in 'inscapes' and 'instresses', his similar need for close, troubled personal searching, and his gift for the minute enjoyment of nature. But unlike Coleridge, Hopkins recorded faithfully, with dates, the daily routine, the weather almost every day, much in the style of a B.B.C. weather report, his engagements—'Breakfast with X', and—inconceivable with Coleridge—a note as to when Oxford Union fees fell due! His methodical entries can be categorized as either secular or religious; Coleridge's never. In other words, for all the many similarities Hopkins's notebooks are a different genre. They are a more systematic account of what Coleridge called 'doings and done-unto's'. Doings and done-unto's interested Coleridge much less than what was going on in the world deeply *within*, or grandly in the universe *without*. The contrast at this point with Hopkins is, I think, fruitful for our understanding of Coleridge.

An eye open for notebooks for some years now has not lit upon any just like Coleridge's. One sees elements in common with Leonardo's, with Baudelaire's journals, with Simone Weil's notebooks, but he is a little like all and like none of them. Simone Weil's bear some resemblances in their wide range of public and private concern, and in approaches through philosophy and religion; but there is no affinity of spirit or style. Simone Weil is of a later generation—angry, aggressive, and positive, where Coleridge is anxious, exploratory, and psychologically inquiring. They both suffered deeply, but Coleridge laughed more often. On first hearing a nightingale in spring he wrote:

22 April, 1826—heard the Nightingales in Widow Cootes' Lane. The Gardner (n.b. so deaf that I was forced to *holler* in his ear) had heard them two days before! [Folio N *f42*]

At the deeper personal levels Baudelaire's *Journals* have more in common with Coleridge's. Day-dreaming, procrastination, resolutions to reform, attempts to cure himself, and above all, a man searching for himself in an acute sense of isolation (for all his many friends), and searching also for anchorage in external relationships, to persons, the physical world, society, science, and trying to discover the principles behind the arts, society —all. A painful sense of *guilt* is a common substratum, but the effect is quite different. Baudelaire did not analyse; he declared himself, wrote in aphorisms, adumbrated subjects, turned a brief paradox with neatness and sharpness. The tone is quite different from Coleridge's tentative questionings, explorations, self-critical qualification piled on qualification, one question leading to another still more basic.

Compare Baudelaire (I quote in Isherwood's translation):

If when a man has fallen into habits of idleness, of day-dreaming and of sloth, putting off his most important duties continually till the morrow, another man were to wake him up one morning with heavy blows of a whip, and were to whip him unmercifully, until he, who was unable to work for pleasure now worked for fear—would not that man, the chastiser, be his benefactor and truest friend? [§ xii, p. 9]

Though Coleridge could not have perpetrated the

notion of any real work induced by fear, he could have had a similar masochistic fantasy. Cf. an entry of 1805:

Of the Blows given by a person to himself, to his hands, breast, or forehead, in the paroxysms of *Self-reproof*—sometimes do they not tend to force the bodily sensations into union with that idea in the mind, which is the dictate of Reason & Duty—so as to make the body itself feel the *condemnation* which the mind feels so deeply?—But I wish to explain fully that self-charged Insincerity, that Histrionism (*Histrio* the Latin for an *Actor on a Stage*) of which the Soul half-accuses itself in many of its efforts at self-condemnation and self-reformation. I have before in my Hints and Notes de Consolatione remarked, that this is a sad Strategem, as it were, of Vice to detain the Prisoner, who is struggling to escape from it, by inspiring Despondency—& in order to avert this from myself and others I would fain shew that this is the natural and necessary feeling that must accompany any and every spirit[ual] Revol[ution] and every incipient change of Habit. . . . [*CN* II 2541]

The 'self-charged insincerity' is authentic Coleridge, and not characteristic of Baudelaire's *Journals*.

One entry not easy to read (as he said in another note, 'I am too much in earnest and in too great restlessness of bodily pain to reduce my words to the rules of Syntax' [Folio N *f83ᵛ*]), revealing a characteristically self-analytical movement of thought, comes out of a lonely moment of illness in 1808:

Ah! dear Book! Sole Confidant of a breaking Heart, whose social nature compels *some* Outlet. I write more unconscious that I am writing, than in my most earnest modes I *talk*—I am not then so unconscious of talking, as when I write in these dear . . . Books, I am of the act of writing—So much so, that even in this last minute or two that I have been writing on my writing, I detected that the former

Habit was predominant—I was only *thinking*. All minds must think by some *symbols*—the strongest minds possess the most vivid Symbols in the Imagination—yet this ingenerates a *want*, πoθον, *desiderium*, for vividness of Symbol: which something that is *without*, that has the property of *Outness* (a word which Berkley preferred to 'Externality') can alone fully gratify / even that indeed not fully—for the utmost is only an approximation to that absolute *Union*, which the soul sensible of its imperfection in itself, of its *Halfness*, yearns after, whenever it exists free from meaner passions, as Lust, Avarice, love of worldly power, passion for distinction in all its forms . . .

Coleridge then runs off the logical and syntactical rails completely, with a slash at Regency routs, the callousness of the rich, the sufferings of the poor and pregnant, the vanity of authors irritated by reviews—as he said, his thoughts 'crowd each other to death'. [*CN* III 3342]

I say, every generous mind not already filled by some one of these passions feels its *Halfness*—it cannot *think* without a symbol—neither can it *live* without something that is to be at once its Symbol, & its *Other half*[1]—(That phrase now so vulgar by the profane use of it was most beautiful in its origin—)—Hence I deduce the habit, I have most unconsciously formed, of *writing* my inmost thoughts—I have not a soul on earth to whom I can reveal them—and yet

'I am not a God, that I should stand alone'

and therefore to you, my passive, yet sole true & kind, friends I reveal them. *Burn you I certainly shall, when I feel myself dying*; but in the Faith, that as the Contents of my mortal frame will rise again, so that your contents will rise with me, as a Phoenix from its pyre of Spice & Perfume. [*CN* III 3325]

The bitterness here was attached to what he took to be

---

[1] See also *CN* II 3026.

Sara Hutchinson's faithlessness, but one notes the resilient spirit rising in him from the ashes. This also is Coleridge.

What then *is* characteristic of his self-searching in the Notebooks? Here he is in Malta in 1805:

It is a subject not unworthy of meditation to myself, what the reason is that these sounds & bustles of Holidays, Fairs, Easter-mondays, & Tuesdays, & Christmas Days, even when I was a Child & when I was at Christ-Hospital, always made me so heart-sinking, so melancholy? Is it, that from my Habits, or my want of money all the first two or three and 20 years of my Life I have been *alone* at such times?— That by poor Frank's dislike of me when a little Child I was even from Infancy forced to be by myself—or rather is it not, that from the distressful specific nature of my ill-health, as well as from all these other causes, & from sundry accidents of my Life, I cannot be happy, but while awakening, enjoying, and giving *sympathy* to one or a few eminently loved Beings, and that when external Joyances call away my attention from these Dreams, which are the poor substitute & wretched Mock-indemnifications of that Sympathy & that Society I *feel* my Hollowness? . . . [*CN* II 2647]

The phrase 'I *feel* my Hollowness!' derives additional force from an entry twenty years later, in Highgate:

Poor—embarrassed—sick—unpatronized, unread— / But (replied the soft consoling Friend) *innocent.*—I felt only as one that recoils—& sinful dust and ashes that I am—groaning under self-reproached inproaches!—*I* innocent?—.—Be thankful still! (repeated the same [. . .] sweet Voice) you are an *innocent* man—Again I draw back but as a little child from a *kind* Stranger, but without letting go of the Stranger's hand / —'You have the childish Heart.—Ah but even in boyhood there was a cold hollow spot, an aching in that heart, when I said my prayers—that prevented my entire union with God—that I could not *give up*, or that would not give *me* up—as if a snake had wreathed around my heart, and at this one spot its Mouth touched at & inbreathed a weak incapability of willing it away— / —'. [Folio N *f7ᵛ*]

A rich entry for the psychiatrists. Or another of 1808:

Told to no one the passion of his Heart / A Hope he had within his Heart, but kept it to himself—he talked of many other things, he talked & tried to think, but always thought of this sweet Hope, a thought still going on / Sometimes he seemed to see it, sometimes he seemed to hear it, according as the feeling or blended with the stirring power of eye or ear, whichever from whatever cause then happ'd to be most active / Just as if this Hope at heart were itself a formal spirit / — [*CN* II 3209]

The last entry (with two short interventions) was sandwiched between a metrical scheme proposed as an improvement on one of Samuel Daniel's, and the following newspaper item:

Lydia Chard, in Finsbury Square, a young Lady of 22— while attending her Mother who had fainted away, caught fire—the servants one screamed, the other fainted / she in vain wrapt herself up in the Carpet Rug—in the confusion a woman came in, & pretending to assist suffered her for near 10 minutes to be burning in her stays &c & then got off having cut away & taken off bothe her pockets / 19 Novem: [*CN* II 3206]

Why this? I feel I must make the point that although we are directing our attention here mainly to the intros-pective entries, it would be a mistake to carry away the impression that Coleridge's notebooks are morbidly self-centred. Quite the contrary.

There is admittedly too much self pity—enough to help one to understand at times the impatience of the

Wordsworths, and others. But surely it is redeemed by candour like this:

Thursday Night, X.   9 Septr 1830.

It is a painful, a mortifying, but even therefore a necessary business, to make strict inquisition into the amiable tendencies of the comparatively best-natured Individuals, as soon as they are loose from the leading-strings of the Universal Reason. . . . Thus, take the yearning to be beloved, the craving for sympathy, in persons of active & constitutional Sensibility: and trace this thro' the craving to become an Object of Sympathy, and in order to this to be at once an Object of Pity & of Admiration—and then watch the day-dreams, that have perhaps been scared & frowned or scoffed away by the awaking Conscience & the re-dawning Light of Reason, in order to detect the little tricks, and tricky imaginations, by which the creaturely Will *subjectively* realizes for itself the sense of being beloved / There are persons for whom Vanity (i.e. Praise, Applause, Admiration) has little or no charm for itself—nay, would be felt as an annoyance—yet who may detect in themselves all the little silly stratagems and hypocrisies of Vanity, when it works as a Means to the excitement of Love & of Sympathy in those whom we wish to love us. It is therefore Selfishness: that is, the Self is not only the starting-point *from*, but the Goal, *to*—which the Soul is working during such moments—and consequently it is a Circuit of Ascent to a Zenith completing itself by a descent to the Nadir— [N 46 *f21*]

The point about persons for whom applause has little charm receives a poignant addition from another entry about ten years earlier. (One remembers that Coleridge was asthmatic or had some similar pulmonary difficulty.)

There is a ~~praise, a hope, a sympathy~~ species of applause scarcely less ~~necessary~~ genial to a ~~man or genius~~ Poet, whether Bard, Musician, or artist, than the vernal warmth to the feathered Songsters during their Nest building or

Incubations—a sympathy, an expressed Hope, that is the ~~May~~ open air in which the Poet breathes, and without which the Sense of Power sinks back on itself like a ~~Sickness~~ sigh heaved up from the tightened Chest of a sick man. [N 21½ f47]

(Mrs. Gillman has written below this entry, Alas! Alas! Alas!)

We see that Coleridge was well aware of the dangers of self-concentration. He is writing about how ' "Evil begets Evil" '—

One error almost compels another / tell one lie tell a hundred / O to show this a priori by bottoming it in all our faculties / & by experience of touching Examples . . .

There follow a few lines in Greek letters which transliterate into a mishmash of Italian, German, English, with a few Greek words; they describe what happens in those half-waking, half-dozing reveries connected in his case with opium and guilt. No translation of that mishmash can convey sharply enough the painful immediacy and intimacy of the manuscript:

He encourages a deception and cerebelline fantasies through the night; awakening into consc[iousness] in the morning early, and sometimes so as not to remain awake, he hopes for a delusion—Then anxiety, stifling breath. [*CN* II 2535]

A hundred entries later he noted that a nervous or perturbed man may carry on his dream into his waking thoughts (where a healthy man cannot) and as it fades he 'has time to watch and compare' [*CN* II 2638], possibly not the Freudian view, but an interesting observation.

Because of his awareness of his own self-deception— and because he saw what he called 'self-centering resolve' in Southey, and 'self-vorticity' in Wordsworth, he believed in 'genuine self-research', to quote the first number of *The Friend*. He thought the study of psychology should not be separated from physiology, 'depriving the former' he said 'of all root and objective truth', and conversely that physiology should not be 'a mere enumeration of facts and phenomena without copula or living form'. He was distressed by the contemporary 'gloomy and hopeless opinions concerning Insanity, with the comparatively low state and the empirical character of the Practice in this department'.

Medicine [he said in 1808] hitherto has been too much confined to *passive* works—as if fevers &c—were the only human calamities. A Gymnastic Medicine is wanting, not a mere recommendation but a system of forcing the Will & *motive faculties* into action. There are a multitude of cases which should be treated as Madness—i.e. the genus Madness should be extended & more classes & species made, in practise, tho' of course, not in name. [*CN* III 3431]

In the reign of George III there was a good deal of public discussion of insanity, but Coleridge's interest was personal. The entry just quoted is the first of several statements about what was called 'madness', in some of which he explicitly refers to himself as potentially a patient for a mental hospital—courageous statements at any time, but much more so 150 years ago than now. Fear of insanity showed itself early, in his undergraduate letters to his brother George about Silas Tomkyn Comberbache. In fact it has been ferretted out[1] that Coleridge was released from the Dragoons on the plea of insanity. It was doubtless well-understood to be

---

[1] By Vera Watson in a letter in *TLS*, 7 July 1950.

a face-saver for officialdom, but letters of his brother George[1] then and later make it clear that the family felt the alternatives were 'mad', or 'bad', and preferred the view that Samuel, the scapegrace of a rising family, was not quite responsible for his actions. The effect on his own shaky opinion of himself is one for speculation. States of mind were a distinct, indeed his main, source of suffering, and though it is not always the popular view of Coleridge to think so, the notebooks put it beyond doubt that he tried to grasp the nettle and to analyse the stings.

For a drug addict such analyses require a maximum heroism. The entries in the notebooks that actually refer to and deal with opium are not (those that escaped censoring scissors) particularly informative. He described himself as 'Chained by a darling passion or *tyrannic* Vice (opium)[2] in Hell, yet with the Telescope of an unperverted Understanding descrying and describing Heaven and the Road thereto to my companions, the Damn'd! O fearful fate! S.T.C.' [*CN* III 3539]. But more interesting than the tyrannic vices are the tyrannic dreams.

The *locus classicus* for Coleridge on sleep and dreaming, his poem *The Pains of Sleep*, is given a rich background in those 'infernal dreams' he recorded in the notebooks. In the Folio Book, more than twenty years after the event, he still recalled one specific dream in the same month as the poem, September 1803. Even in such a moment a self-mocking humour comes out:

---

[1] Some 140 letters now in Victoria College Library, University of Toronto.

[2] Written in his cipher.

26 April 1826. Wednesday Night. This Morning a little
before three suffered one of my most grievous and alarming
‹Scream-› Dreams—and on at length struggling myself
awake found just such a focus of Ferment just above the
Navel as if the Daemon of Aqua Fortis had just closed in
with the Genie Magnesia, or as if a Chocolate Mill were
making a Water-spout dance a reel in dizzy-frisk.—It is
strongly impressed on my mind, that I shall imitate my dear
Father in this as faithfully as Nature imitates or repeats him
in me in so many other points—viz. that I shall die in
sleep / —even as in the Epitaph I composed in my sleep
under the notion that I had died, at an Inn at Edinburgh,
during my Scotch Tour . . .

Here lies poor Col. at length, and without Screaming,
Who died as he had always liv'd—a dreaming!
Shot thro' with pistol by the Gout within,
Alone and all unknown at Embro' in an Inn.

I remember, I awoke from the stimulus of pure vanity from
the admiration of my own fortitude, coolness, and calmness
in bearing my death so heroically—as to be able to compose
my own Epitaph / . [Folio N *f42ᵛ*]

In the next entry he recorded that in his dreams he is
always 'imagining all the wild chambers, Ruins,
Prisons, Bridewells, to be in Hell'—perhaps suggested
he said, by reading Swedenborg on Hell. (Or was it, the
visual aspect of them, by the Piranesi drawings he saw
in Rome? Or, as the birth-trauma theorists would have
it, were those 'wild chambers' a pre-natal memory?) In
any case, no explanation of dreams he had ever heard
satisfied his judgement:

. . . Now I purpose to note down the characteristics of
Dreams, especially my infernal Dreams, as they occur to
me—as so many parts of the Problem to be solved . . . the

Problem itself has never been adequately, no nor even tolerably, stated—.

The first point of course is the Vision itself—that we see without eyes and hear without Ears.—

The second (& which I have never seen noticed) is—that we live without consciousness of Breathing. You never suppose the Men & Women of the Dream to breathe—you do not suppose them *not* to breathe—the thought is wholly *suspended*—and absent from your consciousness.

The third concerns the qualities & relations of Somnial or Morphean Space[1]—which I now must content myself by *Mem*-ming.

The fourth is the spontaneity of the Dream-personages— Each is its own centre—herein so widely differing from the vivid thoughts & half images of poetic Day-dreaming.—In sleep you are perfectly detached from the Dreamatis Personae—& they from you.

The 5th is the whimsical transfer of familiar Names and the sense of Identity and Individuality to the most unlike Forms & Faces. So the Dream, noted almost 30 years ago in one of my Pocketbooks, of Dorothy Wordsworth / and last night of Mrs Gillman.—

Some others I could put down, but it is getting late—& I must defer them.—It is time to be saying my prayers, and to intreat protection 'from the Spirits of Darkness'—a phrase in one of Jer. Taylor's fine Prayers, which I am always *inclined* to retain—tho' the fear of praying what I do not fully believe makes me alter it into—Afflictions of Sleep. S.T.C. [Folio N *f43*]

The subject of Coleridge on dreams is a rich but dangerous one, deserving full treatment by a fully trained analytical imagination, though his accounts of actual dreams are not so numerous as one might expect and wish for, presumably because they were both horrible and monotonously alike. The most recurrent

---

[1] A subject developed later, in N 36 *f4ᵛ*.

type involved pursuit of him by sinister figures, usually female, half-recognized persons, sometimes school friends, phantom-like distorted creatures making attacks on eyes, arms—castration attacks on various parts of his person. He is persuaded that 'the Bites of that little Devil of a Dog, tho' seemingly very sharp, were not actual Pain but a nervous counterfeit'. 'Sometimes, but rarely, I meet with good-natured Folks, tho' even these are commonly afraid to assist one, or turn out hypocrites'. [N 36 $f6^v$] Often the images are recollections of Christ's Hospital[1] and adolescent schoolboy miseries. Dreams of another painful kind were associated, he said, with 'vast water scenery'. He refers also to flying 'or self-shooting' in dreams, . . . 'the immense Elevations of my flights, out of view of all beneath me—and of the prodigious Height of the vast Temples & Palaces, on the Tops of which I alight'. [N 36 $f4^v$]

In a delightful discussion of 'Est quod non est' he speculated as to why his dreams instantly lead to Sara Hutchinson 'as the first waking Thought / no recollection giving a hint of the means, except only that in some incomprehensible manner the whole Dream seems to have been—about her?—nay—perhaps all wild, no form, no place, no incident any way connected with her! What then? Shall I dare say, the whole Dream seems to have been *Her—She*'. [*CN* II 2061]

One can only observe that Coleridge a hundred years later could have become if not a brilliant analyst then an analysand that any analyst might covet.

He often connected his dreaming with bodily posture or local pains, or with external sounds like a watch

[1] 1 1726, 1649, and II 2539.

ticking or Mrs. Coleridge opening a door. Such reflections will be regarded by psychiatrists nowadays as often-
times naive, or completely off the track, even admitting
that in this area one had best not say too dogmatically
what the track is. When Coleridge theorized, using his
own dreams as evidence, he abolished all the old
superstitious thinking about dreams as having any sort
of independent content, and in some tentative way
guessed that an understanding of the dreams of the
night would illuminate hidden mental processes of the
day. In May 1818 he made a fascinating memorandum
entitled 'Language of Dream'.

The language of the Dream = Night, is ⨯ [contrary to]
that of Waking = the Day. It is a language of Images and
Sensations, the various dialects of which are far less different
from each other, than the various Day-Languages of Nations.
Proved even by the Dream Books of different Countries &
Ages.
   2. The images either direct, as when a Letter reminds me
of itself, or symbolic—as Darkness for Calamity. . . .

The entry is too long and complex to quote entire; I
skip to §9:

9. The Conscience—the Unity of Day and Night—Q^y are
there two Consciences, the earthly and the Spiritual? . . .
11. Liver—&c. The passions of the Day as often originate
in the Dream, as the Images of the Dream in the Day. . . .
[*CN* III 4409]

He observed the presence of sexuality in dreams; e.g. in a
fairly late entry (*c.* 1827?) on the complexity of Nature
and its reproductive processes:

Mem.—the objectless imageless Passion of HOPE experienced
in Dreams. Item: the connection of Hope with Sexual

Impulse. For *ΛΥΣΤ* will *hope* when *Reason* would despair.....
[N 59 *f6ᵛ*]

There is no doubt then that Coleridge anticipated
Freud in being aware, more than just dimly, that the
dream carries on the work of the day, and that the conscious daytime life is affected by the activity of the
unconscious and sub-conscious mind of the dreamer.
This is apparent not merely from one passing utterance
on the subject but from many, and it is basic to his
approach not only to the mystery of consciousness but of
genius, and art. His interest in dreams arose from his
interest in the totality of our mental life.

So far as we know he invented the word 'subconsciousness', in describing a vision (not stated to be a
dream) 'enriched by subconsciousness of palpability by
influent recollections of Touch' [*CN* II 2915] an entry of
1806. The first uses of the adjective and adverb, *sub-
conscious* and *subconsciously* are attributed by the *O.E.D.*
to De Quincey in 1832 and 1823; no use of *subconsciousness* is recorded prior to 1879. As Coleridge tried des-
perately to dissuade De Quincey from opium-taking, it
is very likely the subject of dreams with their shiftings of
consciousness was discussed between them. In any case,
with no established vocabulary—perhaps one may say,
unhampered by any prevailing jargon—Coleridge felt
about him for a language, in his attempt at precision in
describing what he did not find described elsewhere.
Here are some groping phrases:

... depths of Being below, & radicative of, all Consciousness
[*CN* I 6];

Man ... how much lies *below* his own Consciousness [his
italics]; [*CN* I 1554];

Viewed in all moods, consciously, uncons[ciously], semi-consc[iously]—[*CN* i 1575];

We find in Shakespeare

Feelings, that never perhaps were attached by us consciously to our own personal Selves [*CN* ii 2086];

the mysterious gradations of Consciousness [*CN* iii 3362];

The province [of the Imagination] is to give consciousness to the Subject by presenting to it its conceptions *objectively*. [*CN* iii 4066]

These are but a small sampling from many such phrases. His remarkable gift for psychological insight and self-analysis (which included sensing its dangers) enabled him to be aware that there are areas of the self outside or 'below his own consciousness', and that these are, creatively, not the least important and valuable sources of energy, e.g. poetic energy, 'the genius in the man of genius'. I should like to quote an entry of 1807 that seems to me to be a fine example of his striving to express the concept of varying levels of consciousness.

I fall asleep night after night watching that perpetual feeling, to which Imagination . . . has given a place and seat of manifestation a shechinah in the heart.—Shall I try to image it to myself, as an animant self-conscious pendulum, continuing for ever its arc of motion by the for ever antici-pation of it?—or like some fairer Blossom-life in the centre of the Flower-polypus, a life within Life, & constituting a part of the Life that includes it? A consciousness within a Consciousness, yet mutually penetrated, each possessing both itself & the other—distinct tho' indivisible! [*CN* ii 2999]

A fully-developed consciousness was, he knew, the weapon against the irrational in all its forms, private and communal,—against superstitions, cheap nostrums, fears and hatreds, and all the social injustices that are their heirs.

'For all things that surround us, and all things that happen unto us, have (each doubtless its own providential purpose, but) all one common final cause: namely, the increase of Consciousness, in such wise, that whatever part of the terra incognita of our nature the increased consciousness discovers, our will may conquer and bring into subjection to itself under the sovereignty of reason.'[1] This was written in 1816, long before Kierkegaard and Freud.

He himself continued to exercise and increase his consciousness to the end of his life with an integrity constantly probed and tested. One last illustration from his old age, which displays also that modest self-persiflage that must have been one of his endearing gentle charms:

Important Memorandum, Tuesday 12 Jany 1830.
Caveat Senescens

On this day I felt myself sufficiently recovered from the last severe Relapse to venture out and dine and spend the Evening at my old School and Form-fellow at Christ's Hospital, Mr Steele's, at the Bottom of the Hill, in Kentish Town. . . . And an excellent Dinner, and a quiet social comfortable day we enjoyed—and I returned in the Carriage with Mrs G. and Miss Ingram (for I had, avoiding, however, the slipperiness of the snow-frozen boy-slidden Hill, walked *thither* down the Dutchess's Lane) . . .—After Tea and Coffee, Susan, Miss Ingram, James Gillman and George Steele being at the Piano, I sate down (—for the first time some twelve months) to a Rubber of Whist, Mrs Gillman my Partner—against Mr Steele & Mr Gillman. And it [is] this

[1] *The Statesman's Manual* in *Lay Sermons* ed. R. J. White in *The Collected Works of Samuel Taylor Coleridge*, p. 89.

that is the subject and occasion of this Memorandum. Tho'
I gave all attention that depended on my Will to the Game
—I trumped Tricks which my Partner had already won—
played a Trump when the only other (I might have known)
was in my Partner's Hand, played the last trump, so as to
destroy the (but for that) certainty of my Partner's making a
long sequence—in short, I both played and felt exactly as I
have often observed very old Persons play, in the decay of
their Faculties.—

Now this,
Tuesday Night, Jany 12th, 1830,
was the first instance in which my own Mind has been
rendered conscious of the Decay of mental powers coming
on with decay of body and elanguescence of bodily Life—
and it has begun just where it might have been expected to
exhibit its first symptoms, i.e. on those directions of the
mental powers in which they had always been the weakest—
Now with me the peccant and weak part has always been in
the application of the sense and judgements to outward
things, in the moment of their presence and during the
period of their Succession. In the application of my Mind to
Thoughts, either in their renewal or their combination, or
in the appreciative and inferential Acts, I have hitherto
traced no decline. But the decay, no doubt, will eat inward
from the surface, in which the caries or necrosis with me has
commenced; . . . Now when in my case the Decay thus
commenced has penetrated inward to the power that con-
verses with Thoughts, to the Subjective Faculties, it is only
too probable that like the good Archbishop of Toledo
[Granada][1] in Gil Blas, I may, by the working of the decay
itself, be unconscious of it, and incredulous. With this view,
under the admonition of this fore-bodement I have made
this Memorandum—and shall desire Mr Green and M^rs
Gillman to take a note that I have so done, and of the

[1] The reference is to Book VII of *Gil Blas* in Chapter 3 of which Gil
Blas is employed as his censor by the Archbishop of Granada, only to be
dismissed in Chapter 4, for performing his duty.

Number of the Fly-Catcher in which this, my 'Caveat
Senescens' Memorandum, is to be found—in order that
when the one or the other exerts, as I fervently beseech, hope
and trust that they will not be deterred from doing, the
trying but most needful duty of true and enduring Friends
by admonishing me, that in such or such a composition, or
that in such or such lengthy talkings, the decaying energy
betrays itself—and I am becoming tiresome when I might
tho' no longer able to amuse or instruct, remain neutral in the
becoming and natural quietness of Old Age (which is not a
mere matter of years)—then should I appear doubtful, this
Memorandum may be recalled to my Memory—and the
experiment may perhaps with this assistance prove less un-
availing than happened in the instance of Gil Blas and the
eloquent Archbishop of Toledo (Granada).— [N 44ff 34]

'Our intellectual life', he said in a lecture on Shakespeare, is passed 'not so much in acquiring new facts,
as in acquiring *a distinct consciousness*'. According to
Coleridge, Consciousness is something which can be
developed; we must learn to be aware so far as possible
of its content and its limitations. Increasing consciousness, he held, would drive out fear and carry us into the
future—and this is what I mean by Coleridge grasping
his own nettle.

In the next lecture I should like to try to present some
aspects of what Coleridge's 'increased consciousness'
discovered in the human life around him.

II

THE SELF AND OTHERS, AND SOME PRINCIPLES OF EDUCATION

In the first lecture I tried to demonstrate that Coleridge's notebooks lay open to us his extraordinary efforts to understand the psyche, and that his subtle awareness came not from books, not only intellectually—of course thence also—but from his own pulses. We see him sometimes gropingly sometimes more firmly describing psychological experiences: the subconscious and pre-conscious states of mind, the work of dreams, the emotional elements in forgetfulness and slips of the pen; in fact in many areas in life Coleridge was aware of sub-jective variations where many of his contemporaries e.g., Sir James Mackintosh, Robert Southey, and Coleridge's own brothers, were still 'facts are facts' men, quite untroubled by such undercurrents. As it has taken more than a hundred years for us to begin to catch up with Coleridge, we should not be surprised at them. We now have an access, owing to Freud and the revolution in thought consequent on his work, that Coleridge's immediate editors and expositors did not have. Few if any of them—perhaps his daugher Sara, by the flickering light of her own similar sensibility, and per-haps, partially F. D. Maurice—saw that the fulcrum of Coleridge's thought was psychological. Because of its daring, and delicacy and uncertainty, for Coleridge lacked the technical vocabulary that came later, the notebooks are the place where he tried out many of these strange 'cogitabilia', and are the prime source for them. Having seen them there, we re-read the more formal works with fuller understanding of his meaning.

Coleridge was fascinated by the multiple phenomena of human illusions, being acutely aware, as I have suggested, of self-deception in himself as well as in others. His entrance to worlds within worlds did not alleviate his condition or make him suffer the less;[1] it did help, however, to produce *The Ancient Mariner* and *Christabel* and *Kubla Khan*; it may well be the mainspring of their continuing vitality and of what is sometimes called their 'magical' power. Much as I am tempted to follow that track, I shall stick to the notebooks themselves, which do not often directly discuss or present the poems; a few implications for the poetry will appear here and there.

What I should like to attempt in this lecture is to see in what directions Coleridge's self-conscious imagination turned when it looked outwards, towards human kind.

The extent of his exertion and projection of himself into the broad world of human affairs is not always sufficiently to the fore in our over-all views of him. For this reason William Walsh's study of his contribution to educational theory in *The Use of Imagination* (1959) is helpful and important, as are two studies of Coleridge's political theories by Carl Woodring[2] and David Calleo.[3] Coleridge's pamphlets in 1818 in support of Peel's

---

[1] See e.g. *CN* iii 4166.
[2] *Politics in the Poetry of Coleridge* (1961).
[3] *Coleridge and the Idea of the Modern State* (1966).

legislation to curb the exploitation of children in the cotton factories were very astute and forceful, and apparently influential. We know Coleridge, too, as one of the best leader writers of his day, when he worked for Daniel Stuart on the *Morning Post* and the *Courier*. Germs and fragments of all these activities are to be found in the notebooks, and much more having to do with man as citizen and member of the human race. For example, here is an entry on pollution:

> 1 March, 1832—
> Every Epidemic Disease, every epidemic or endemic [?imparted] should awaken us to the deep interest, which every man of every country has in the well-being of all men; and in the consequent progressive *humanization* of the Surface & with it the atmosphere of the Planet itself. Only for our present and narrow view. Moral & physical aesthetic terms. —As Man, so the World he inhabits. It is his business and duty to *possess* it, to rule it, to assimilate it to his own higher Nature. If instead of this he suffers himself to be possessed, ruled, and assimilated by it, he becomes an animal who like the African Negro, or the South American Savage, is a mischief to Man even by neglect of his functions as a man. The neglected Earth steams up poisons that TRAVEL. [Folio N *f79ᵛ*]

There is something alarmingly prescient at times about the imaginations of those impractical poets.

Thus we see that Coleridge's poetry and prose, like his notebook memoranda, took root in his minute inspection not only of the inner self, but of external relations; and the two were never severed from each other but seen always in some dynamic tension of opposition or reconciliation. In 1808 he was asking some of the questions Carlyle was to ask later:

If it were asked of me to justify the interest, ... the majority of the best and noblest minds feel in the great questions—Where am I? What and for what am I? What are the duties, which arise out of the relations of my Being to itself as heir of futurity, and to the World which is its present sphere of action and impression?—I would compare the human Soul to a Ship's Crew cast on an unknown Island (a fair Simile: for these questions could not suggest themselves unless the mind had previously felt convictions, that the present World was not its whole destiny and abiding Country)—what would be their first business? Surely, to enquire ‹what the Island was? in what Latitude?› what ships visited that Island? when? and whither they went?—and what chance that they should take off first one, & then another?—and after this—to think, how they should maintain & employ themselves during their stay—& how best stock themselves for the expected voyage, & procure the means of inducing the Captain to take them to the Harbour, which they wished to go to?—

The moment, when the Soul begins to be sufficiently self-conscious, to ask concerning itself, & its relations, is the first moment of its *intellectual* arrival into the World—Its *Being*—enigmatic as it must seem—is posterior to its *Existence*.—Suppose the shipwrecked man stunned, & for many weeks in a state of Ideotcy or utter loss of Thought & Memory—& then gradually awakened. [*CN* III 3593]

His starting-point for what he called 'our common need for connexions' was candidly and deliberately taken in the Self itself. E.g. in the autumn of 1803 when he was thirty years old he confided to his Notebook 4 the first hint of *Biographia Literaria*:

Seem to have made up my mind to write my metaphysical works as *my Life* & *in* my Life intermixed with all the other events or history of the mind & fortunes of S. T. Coleridge. [*CN* I 1515]

The self might be so used, because even this early he had found in it a great deal that was not merely individual.

In his first published collection, *Poems on Various Subjects*, in 1796, he justified egotism in certain kinds of poems. His whole Preface is in fact full of psychological insights, but the main argument is that egotism in poetry can give pleasure and solace from pain, through the healing by communication of our feelings to one another. The reverse sort of egotism, 'which would reduce the feelings of others to an identity with our own' he naturally dismissed as beneath contempt. (Elsewhere he called it 'he-goat-ism'.) But the real attack was launched against those egotists who try to conceal their egotism by avoiding being egotists in speech.

. . . With what anxiety every fashionable author avoids the word *I*!—now he transforms himself into a third person, —'the present writer'—now multiplies himself and swells into '*we*'—and all this is the watchfulness of guilt. Conscious that this said *I* is perpetually intruding on his mind and that it monopolizes his heart, he is prudishly solicitous that it may not escape from his lips.

This disinterestedness of phrase is in general commensurate with selfishness of feeling: men old and hackneyed in the ways of the world are scrupulous avoiders of Egotism.

A few years later he was still worrying about egotism:

Those . . . who from prudence abstain from Egotism in their writings, are still Egotists among their friends— / It would be unnatural effort not to be so / & Egotism in such cases is by no means offensive to a kind & discerning man—

Suppressed egotism, easily becomes '*contempt*, which is the concentrated Vinegar of Egotism'. [*CN* 1 904]

There is absolutely no vinegar in Coleridge's own egotism.

The egotism discussed in impersonal generalities is, however, comprehended intimately, not only because he had suffered from it in others, but because he was well aware of the S. T. Coleridge who was to appear in Max Beerbohm's 'Table Talking' cartoon. 'There are two sorts of talkative fellows whom it would be injurious to confound, and I, S. T. Coleridge, am the latter', he said, and recounted how, going on endlessly in circles, 'I break against the shore of my Hearer's patience, or have my Concentricals dashed to nothing by a Snore— that is my ordinary mishap'. At Malta, however, 'I have earned the general character of being a quiet well meaning man, rather dull indeed—& who would have thought that he had been a *Poet*!' [*CN* II 2372]

Egotistic Talk *with me* very often the effect of my Love of the Persons to whom I am talking / My Heart is talking of them / I cannot talk continuously of them to themselves—so I seem to be putting into their Heart the same continuous- ness as to me, that is in my own Heart as to them.—[*CN* I 1772]

This is *echt* Coleridge. Even Hazlitt, disciple turned enemy, in *The Spirit of the Age* defended him. 'Mr. Coleridge talks of himself, without being an egotist, for in him the individual is always merged in the abstract and general.'

Coleridge himself expressed it this way:

I remember [he was to say some years later] . . . when first I saw the connection between Time, and the being resisted; Space and non-resistance—or unresisted Action— that if no object met, stopped, or opposed itself to my sight, ear, touch, or sensitive power, tho' it were but my own pulse rising up against my own thumb, I could have no sense of Time; & but for these, or the repetition of these in the reproductive Memory or Imagination, should have no Time. . . . For in truth, Time and Self are in a certain sense one and the same thing: since only by meeting with, so as to be resisted by, *Another*, does the Soul become a *Self*. What is Self-consciousness but to know myself at the same moment that I know another, and to know myself by means of knowing another, and vice-versa, an other by means of & at the moment of knowing my Self. Self and others are as necessarily interdependent as Right and Left, North and South. [N 23 *ff* 31ᵛ–32]

This is an entry of the 1820s. About twenty years earlier he had expressed the last thought more emotionally:

My nature requires another Nature for its support, & reposes only in another from the necessary Indigence of its Being.—Intensely similar, yet not the same; or may I venture to say, the same indeed, but dissimilar, as the same Breath sent with the same force, the same pauses, & with the same melody pre-imaged in the mind, into the Flute and the Clarion shall be the same Soul diversely incarnate. [*CN* 1 1679]

'Similar, yet not the same', or if 'the same, indeed, yet dissimilar.' In an early entry, referring to the conflicts in human societies, he asked, 'Why is difference linked with hatred?' [*CN* 1 1376] His answer ultimately was, from lack of adequate consciousness of self.

An uncompleted entry headed 'Imagination' in the Folio notebook,[1] begins treating this subject with an analysis of the primary bounds of the 'I'—and the necessity of being conscious of the identity of knowing

---

[1] Folio N *ff* 15–15ᵛ.

and being that constitutes it. Presumably lack of consciousness of this 'self-position' of the I, inhibits the I's sense of the truth both about itself and all others. 'Selfishness implies the want of Self-Consciousness', he says, citing Colonel Delmour's character in Susan Ferrier's novel, *The Inheritance*. A late entry beginning 'There are many Shames' concludes with this:

Unless a man understand his own heart, it is impossible that he should have insight into the Hearts of other men. And how should *he* understand his own Heart who is afraid or ashamed to look *into* it, yea even to look *at* it? [N 51 *f6*]

Coleridge did not need the experience of the psychoanalyst's couch to tell him that the real sources of emotional suffering are not always the surface ones; they must be searched for, sometimes the 'obscure feelings' of a lifetime, difficult to clarify, and perhaps even infantile. The 'form and limits' of the suffering must be sought out, to solve the problem. The Soul is thus not at once given its complete entity, he thought; it has to be awakened to learn to develop its potential. Increasing our consciousness of self is a moral obligation, because the lack of it can be harmful to other persons, and destructive of that 'continuousness' of interlocking and constructive relationships that is essential to the good society.

In the days of Napoleon the figure of the tyrant came readily to mind, *ex hypothesi* an extrovert type without self-inspection, and Coleridge made numerous uses of the image displaying its destructive rationalizings. In an entry of 1803 he traced certain elements in the tyrant syndrome to childhood and disease, smallpox, for instance, which was thought to cause impotence.

The vices of tyrannical great men very closely connected with their vices as Striplings, at Schools & Universities.— Tiberius. Lord Lonsdale. P-x. Impotence.—Painful Sensation and Loss of Hope = castration of the self-generating Organ of the Soul / —Continuousness a true Foliation.— [*CN* I 1552]

'Continuousness' here is the foliation vertically from one generation to the next. Children being 'the stock of Hope', an impotent man senses the loss of his future, in the *gestaltist* sense [*CN* II 2549]. (Coleridge gives various indications of *gestalt* concepts.) 'My Neighbour is my *other* Self, *othered* by Space—my old age is to my youth an other Self, *othered* by Time—'. [*CN* III 4017] The horizontal continuum in society is often broken by powerful men, from their self-important ignorance of themselves and other persons.

Friday, Nov. 23, 1804
One of the heart-depraving Habits & Temptations of men in power, as Governors, &c &c is to make *instruments* of their fellow-creatures—& the moment, they find a man of Honor & Talents, instead of loving & esteeming him, they wish to *use him* / hence that self-betraying side & down look of cunning &c—and they justify & inveterate the habit by believing that every individual who approaches has selfish designs upon them. [*CN* II 2271]

That entry came out of his experiences as a diplomat in Malta. The worst thing one human being can do to another, in his view, is to treat him as something less than an autonomous human being with powers and rights. 'Respect the individuality of your friend' he counsels, or your child—or any opponent or employee.

In all sorts of contexts Coleridge urges the importance of good 'habits of feeling'. [*CN* II 2435] What is needed is educated emotions as well as the educated intellect. Particular actions may be good or bad, but it is not what we do, but what we are that matters. The man makes the motives. Bad actions do not necessarily imply a bad man, nor by the same reasoning, do virtuous acts necessarily mean a truly good man. Good or bad actions equally may lack that creative factor of imagination related to awareness of self, that creative imaginative energy that 'brings the whole soul of man into activity'.[1] The point can be illustrated by two entries about Southey, and it gains something from the privacy of memoranda written for no other purpose than self-clarification:

Prodigious Efficacy in preventing Quarrels and Interruptions of Friendship among Mankind in general, but especially among young warm-hearted men, would the habitual Reflection be, that the Almighty will judge us not by what we *do* but by what we *are*. . . .—Apply this now to my former Quarrel with Southey.—On what ground, in the first place, did I form a friendship with him? Because our pursuits were similar, our final aspirations similar; & because I saw plainly, that compared with the mass of men Southey was pure in his *Habits*, habitually indignant at oppression, *habitually* active in behalf of the oppressed, both by exertion & by self-sacrifice.—Not that he was Perfection; but because he was a far better man, than the vast majority of the young men, whom I knew. What had I to oppose to all this?—An alteration of any of these *Habits?* Had Southey ceased to be Southey?—No. What then?—Why, one or two *Actions*—done under the warping & amid the bedimming Glare of Passion, & interpreted by me, my own mind being in that State—Actions which probably the faulty parts of my own *character* had had no small share in producing—actions, to

[1] *Biographia Literaria*, Chapter XIV.

which Southey had been led in some measure by the very same Blunder with regard to me, which I fell into with regard to him / —viz—brooding over some one *action* of mine, an *action* of *words*, such as it had been *reported* to him perhaps—at all events, such as he had *conceived* it to be—at a time when it was quite impossible for us to think with even tolerable calmness & dispassionateness of each other, either for Evil or for Good.—If either of us in some moment when from some accidental association a feeling of old Tenderness had revisited our Hearts, had paused—& asked our selves— Not what C. has *done*? or what has S. *done*?—but—Well! in spite of this—a bad business, to be sure—but spite of it— what *is* C. or S. on the whole? If I go to him in Distress, would not all this Resentment vanish? would he not divide his last Shilling with me! . . . [*CN* 1 1605]

There is more, but this is enough to give the tone of Coleridge's efforts in October 1803, when the Southeys had taken up residence in Greta Hall, to work himself out of resentment. Three months later he was still in conflict:

The character of Australis [Southey] a striking Illustration of the Basis of Morals. With truth, & with the warm coloring of one who feels the Truth, detail his Life, as a History, & the Tenor of his Life, as a system of Habits of his never once stumbling Temperance, his unstained Chastity from his Infancy to the present Hour, . . . Industry, & vigorous Perseverance in his Pursuit, the worthiness & dignity of these Pursuits, his Liberality & fatherly conduct to his Brothers & Relatives—& for their sake how he submits to *review & Job*, yet by unexampled Industry can do this & yet do more than almost any other man, in the Subjects of his Choice & Ambition / his punctuality in all things—he inflicts none of those small Pains & Discomforts, which your irregular men scatter about them, & vice versa, bestows all the pleasures which regular correspondence, & a *reliability* in all things great & small can give / —he is kind to his

servants, & he is more than kind—he is *good* to them / Bella
for instance / —all his works subserve Humanity, & the
great cause of Peace, Equality, & pure Religion—and above
all, of domestic Fidelity & Attachments of which as a
Husband (& no doubt, he will as a Father) he is himself in
his real Life a Pattern in the eyes of ordinary good men / —
All this Australis *does*, & if all Goodness consists in definite,
observable, & rememberable *Actions*, Australis is only not
perfect, his good Actions so many, his unad[mirable] ones
so few, & (with one or two exceptions) so venial. But now
what is Australis? I can tell you, what he is NOT. He is not a
man of warmth, or delicacy of Feeling, HE IS NOT self-
oblivious or self-diffused, or acquainted with his own nature:
& when warped by Resentment or Hatred, not incapable of
doing base actions, at all events most *very*, or *damn'd*,
indelicate actions, without hesitation at the moment, or any
after-remorse. . . .

The entry continues in a mixture of Latin and Greek to
refer resentfully to past episodes involving malice and
anger that need not distract us here, all of which,
Coleridge says,

follows from an unfathoming (and not only self-unfathomed,
but even self-unsounded, Spirit). The smiles, the emanations,
the perpetual Sea-like Sound & Motion of Virtuousness
which is Love, is wanting— / He is a clear handsome piece
of Water in a Park, moved from without. . . . [*CN* 1 1815]

Allowing for the irritations of being housemate with
a paragon of regularity and rectitude, and for the
jealousy and envy from practical comparisons—as to
marital happiness, literary productivity, and financial
success—one nevertheless takes Coleridge's point,
whether strictly applicable to Southey or not, of the
importance of self-fathoming and self-sounding to the

creation of loving relationships as opposed to dutiful
ones.

That Coleridge imposed on himself—perhaps too
often—the self-inspection he demanded of others is
illustrated by many entries. I choose from this same
period a few sentences about relations with Wordsworth.
Interestingly Coleridge depersonalized the argument
for himself by referring to himself as 'A', Wordsworth
as 'B':

A. thought himself unkindly used by B.—he had exerted
himself for B. with what warmth! honoring, praising B.
beyond himself.—&c &c—B. selfish—feeling all Fire respecting every Trifle of his own—quite backward to poor
A.— . . . This is a very, very dim Sketch / but the *Fact* is
stated.—Then, A. took himself to Task respecting *B*.—It is
very true, that B. is not so zealous as he might be, in some
things—and overzealous for himself—But what *is* he on the
whole? What compared with the mass of men?—It is
astonishing how powerfully this Medicine acted—how
instantly it effected a cure / one wakeful Hour's serious
Analysis—& the Light thrown upon the former Subject had
a great Share in this—for one important part of the Process
in the growth of Envy is the Self-degradation (a painful selfish
referent Feeling) consequent on the first consciousness of the
pang—the Obscurity & Darkness of mind from ignorance
of the Cause—dim notion that our nature is suddenly
altered for the worse. &c &c.—Deeplier than ever do I see
the necessity of understanding the whole complex mixed
character of our Friend—as well as our own . . .

He then wondered if he had mixed up Envy with some
other feeling—

. . . The same sort of Pain I have distinctly felt, at Mr. Pitt's
being the Author of the Irish Union, deemed by me a great

& wise measure / & introducing a subversion of my *Theory* of Pitt's Contemptibility. Yet it would be strange to say, I envied Mr. Pitt?

After more argument he decided that in himself '. . . This seems a Vice of personal Uncharitableness, not Envy.'[1] And finally, still unlabyrinthing himself in the same entry, he said:

Let me re-ennumerate. [1] A. had been dwelling on the faulty parts of B.'s character. . . . These views of A.'s understanding were *just* on this point, only that they had been *exclusive*: occasioned by [2] A. having been himself deeply wounded by B.'s selfishness. . . . [3] A. had been long, long idle owing perhaps in part to his Idolatry of B. . . . 4. A. hears of some new Poems of B.—& feels little painful shrinking back at the Heart . . . —& 5. a disposition to do something to surpass B. . . . —on the whole I suspect the Feeling to have been mere Resentment.—[*CN* i 1606]

It seems only fair occasionally to show that Coleridge could practise as well as preach.

It is from such notes as these on envy (and they are a paradigm for his way with jealousy, pride, vanity, and many other weaknesses) that one understands Coleridge's desperate anxiety to sift through the layers upon layers of conscious and less than fully conscious feelings, fighting not only all the ordinary human tendency to self-flattering illusions but those compounded by the defences and self-deceptions of the lonely neurotic turned drug addict. Rather in the fashion of Jeremy Taylor he saw that to many of us our weaknesses may look like virtues—to ourselves. For example, we may

[1] Cf. an interesting note on some backlash effects from envy, in *CN* ii 2830.

proffer sympathy when really all we are doing is giving
ourselves the pleasure of seeming agreeable:

> The first great requisite is absolute *Sincerity*. Falsehood &
> Disguise are *miseries* & misery-makers, under whatever
> strength of sympathy & desire to prolong happy Thoughts
> *in others* for their sake and my own only as sympathizing with
> theirs it may originate / all sympathy not consistent with
> acknowledged Virtue is but disguised Selfishness—[*CN* III
> 3509]

In 1805, harking back to the memorandum about
envy being perhaps resentment, he refers to our natural
'uneasiness at a non-harmony' in persons, 'that deep
intuition of our oneness—is it not at the bottom of many
of our faults as well as Virtues?'. [*CN* II 2471] Coleridge
had not heard the phrases, 'emotional conflict', or 'split
personality', or 'identity problem', but of the existence
of the reality he was well aware. He knew that human
beings should function, as he held poems did, by a
unified reconciliation of the parts to the whole. What he
said about the ends of human communication, socially,
is very like what he said about poetry, when as here he
was feeling his way towards defining it:

> What if we say—the communication of our Thoughts and
> feelings so as to produce excitement by sympathy, for the
> purpose of immediate pleasure, the most pleasure from each
> part [i.e. each individual] that is compatible with the largest
> possible sum of pleasure from the whole [i.e. the friends,
> family, the social unit whatever it is.] [*CN* III 3827]

He tried again and again in this entry to define poetry
and each time, if for 'parts' we read 'individuals', and
for 'whole' 'society', he might be describing human
institutions.

'And whatever calls into consciousness the greatest number of these faculties in due proportion & perfect harmony with each other is the noblest Poem', or as we may legitimately transpose it—the noblest human society in which the needs of each are reconciled with the requirements of a unified whole. I do not think it is stretching Coleridge's thought, or detracting from the original intention as directed towards poetry, to think of this as a description of the good society.

Certainly the pattern of necessary self-conscious reconciliations through the exercise of imagination in Coleridge's thought is common to both poetry and society. And to much else. Because he was aware that the problems of such reconciliations, even within one individual, may begin in infancy, he was passionately devoted to children and to education. His sympathy for children was, out of his own acute miseries (and pleasures) as a child, highly empathetic. He loved to observe children, but it amounted to more than observation. When he noticed 'A boy sucking an Icicle with what affectionate Remembrance of a Lollipop' [*CN* I 1805] he was surely enjoying the remembrance of his own such oral satisfactions. A less cheerful identification was made on the eve of his departure, in considerable desolation of spirits, for Malta. (It should be remembered that after his father's death Coleridge spoke of himself as an orphan, a feeling accentuated by his place in the family, his mother's disposition, and the Bluecoat School uniform.) He wrote, in no apparent context:

A ~~parent~~ Mother dying of a contagious Disease unable to give or receive the last Embrace to her Orphan Child. [*CN* II 1991]

His frequent and tender returns in dreams and day-
dreams, as well as in his poems, to the image of the
infant at the mother's breast, show how clearly he had
carried on 'the feelings of Childhood into the powers of
Manhood, [had] combine[d] the Child's sense of
wonder and novelty with the Appearances which every
day for perhaps forty years had rendered familiar'.[1] One
of the clearest examples of this retention of infant feelings comes in an entry, very vivid and personal, describing the moment of falling asleep. It is a complex
entry having to do with his love for Sara Hutchinson
(with the cogent words in Greek, Italian, and German)
involving the pillow-breast-infant images of an early
love poem, a pun in Greek, seas and ships and English
spoken with the Devonshire accent of his childhood, and
ending with what in some schools of thought is uterine
imagery.

O what vision (μαστοι) as if my Cheek and Temple were
lying on me gale o' mast on—Seele meines Lebens! & I sink
down the waters, thro' Seas & seas—yet warm, yet a Spirit
— / Pillow = mast high / oi. [*CN* I 1718]

Mastoi is the Greek for breasts, *megalomaston* for large-
breasted, and *hoi* is also a Devon pronunciation of 'high'.
Self-consciousness can probably not go much farther
back into the deeps of yearning recollection and percep-
tion than that.[2] I quote the entry to make clear the
intensity behind Coleridge's awareness of and ability to
articulate infantile fantasies, for we already know how

[1] This ability he said was 'the character and privilege of Genius and
one of the marks which distinguish Genius from Talents' (*Friend* (*CC*) I
109).
[2] See also *CN* I 1414.

his introspection could also issue in outgoing thoughts. It is surely one of his greatnesses as a poet, as illustrated for instance in *Dejection: an Ode*. He began with dark skies, and

> A stifled, drowsy, unimpassioned grief,
> Which finds no natural outlet, no relief

and after an inspection of loneliness and dejection un-paralleled in English poetry, he closed with a beautiful turn of thought outwards towards his beloved Sara Hutchinson,

> May all the stars hang bright above her dwelling . . .
> Joy lift her spirit, joy attune her voice.

Such loving intelligent outgoingness is not necessarily reconcilable with a tendency towards regressive, infan-tile recollections, as we know. And Coleridge could behave as childishly as anyone at times. But he could also extend himself imaginatively outwards from what in one version of *Frost at Midnight* he referred to as 'these wild reliques of our childish Thought', to become 'the great English poet of childhood', as the late critic, Oliver Elton called him. In his poems the references to babes, infants, and children, number nearly four hundred; the references to mothers (often in conjunction with children) about two hundred and fifty. The frequent desire to turn such material into poetry is significant in itself.

To trace the if not absolute birth yet the growth & endur-ancy of Language from the Mother talking to the Child at her Breast—O what a subject for some happy moment of deep feeling, and strong imagination.—[Sara! Sara!] O those dear [children!] [*CN* II 2352]

Earlier he had observed that Hartley 'seemed to learn to talk by touching his mother' [*CN* I 838]. Touch is itself affected (he noticed Derwent) '*by taste* at first—then about 5 months old they go from the Palate to the hand—& are fond of feeling what they have tasted— / Association of the Hand with the Taste—till the latter by itself recalls the former—& of course, with volition. March 24, 1801.' [*CN* I 924] Derwent at this time was six months old. The importance of the hand is developed later in an entry on 'The imperfection of the organs by which we seem to unite ourselves with external things', substantially on analysis of the erotogenic zones. [*CN* II 2399]

In an entry of 1818, after a collection of lecture notes based partly on a recollection of Schelling's 'On the relation of the formative arts to Nature',[1] he wrote:

N.b. the seeming Identity of Body and Mind in Infants, and thence the loveliness of the former—the commencing separation in Boyhood—the *struggle* of equilibrium in youth—from thence onward the Body first indifferent, then demanding the translucency of the mind not to be worse than indifferent—and finally, all that presents the Body as Body almost of a *recremental* (εξ) nature.—[*CN* III 4398]

In the light of this summary of personal crises, elsewhere described more fully in the notebooks,[2] it is not only moving, but also explanatory of Coleridge's sympathy with the young and erring—like Henry Gillman, or his own sons—to find as his last paragraph, in the lecture

[1] This entered largely, but perhaps not so exclusively as has been thought, into lecture notes edited after Coleridge's death as his essay 'On Poesy or Art'. Cf. *CN* III 4397 and n.

[2] See also, e.g., *CN* II 2398.

notes just referred to, this remark, quite unrelated to Schelling:

> To the idea of Life Victory or Strife is necessary—As Virtue [lies] not in the absence of vicious Impulses but in the overcoming of them / so Beauty not in the absence of the Passions, but on the contrary—it is heightened by the sight of what is conquered . . . [*CN* III 4397]

Surely this is the comment of a compassionate man. In this context there is another touching entry, possibly a draft for a conversation with adolescent Hartley, in which STC used himself and his own weaknesses as 'all that should be like a voice from Heaven to warn you'.

> While you are what your Father ever has been, dwell on the foolish, perplexing, imprudent, dangerous, & even immoral conduct of promise-breach in small things, of want of punctuality, of procrastination in all its shapes & disguises.—Force men to reverence the dignity of your moral Strength, in & for itself—seeking no excuses or palliations from Fortune, or Sickness, or a too full mind that in opulence of conception over-rated its powers of application / —But if your Fate, should be different . . . [*CN* III 4188]

and so he went on because it was one of the horrors of his life that his own personality, and more particularly his marital failure, might be injurious to his children. His frequent references to children as 'the secreting-organ of Hope[1] in the great organized Body of the whole Human Race' betray his own anxiety. But it goes without saying that his interest in education was broad and

---

[1] *Hope* was perhaps the most important word in Coleridge's vocabulary. To consult the *Concordance* to his poems again, it appears there, including all forms of it, more than 300 times.

general, not just parental. He was alive to the subject as he was reading the Bible, for instance:

The Jewish Rabbis (according to the Thalmud) anathe-matized a Village having 30 Houses, which did not maintain a School. It has struck me as curious that there are no allusions to Children's Schools in the Gospels or even to the instruction of Children in any way. [Folio *N f95*]

His injunction to revere 'the Individuality of your friend' applied with double force to all children. The child must be regarded as a child, not as a little adult, but with real respect for his powers; he needs to be taught how to develop these powers, not to be stuffed with information. Coleridge was enthusiastic about Dr. Bell's 'Madras System' of education, a progressive system of his day, because of the room it allowed for the child's initiative and growth, but he was no believer in a slack permissiveness. His understanding of the child's feelings in the process—the need for secure authority, and secure affection, as well as an inviolate self—shows not only a remarkable delicacy, but a characteristic trick of holding many diverse considerations in mind simultaneously—the need of parents, for instance, for defences against irritation. He quoted some gentle mis-guided person who had evidently objected to a reproof of a child:

Of Education—'O; it is but an infant! 'tis but a child—he will be better as he grows older—O! she'll grow ashamed of it'.
This is but way-wayriness—Grant all this!—and that *they* will *outgrow* these particular actions, yet with what HABITS of *feeling* will they arrive at youth & manhood—Especially, with regard to obedience—how is it possible that

they should struggle against the boiling passions of youth by means of obedience to their own Conscience, who are to meet the dawn of Conscience with the broad Meridian of Disobedience & Habits of Self-willedness? Besides—when are the rebukes, the chastisements to commence in this mode—Why!—about 9, or 10 perhaps, when—for the Father at least—it is less a plaything—when therefore the anger is not healed up in the child mind, either by its own infant versatility & forgetfulness, or by after Caresses—when everything is remembered individually, & a sense of injustice felt—For the boy very well remembers the different treatment when he [was] a child—he does not look back on his last year's self as on a Child—but what has been so long permitted, becomes a Right to him—Far better in such a case to have them sent off to others, a strict Schoolmaster, than to breed that contradiction of feeling toward the same person which subverts the very *principle* of our Impulses / — Whereas in a tender yet obedience-exacting & improvement-enforcing Education—tho' very gradually, & by small doses at a time—yet always going on, yea, even from a twelve-month old—at 6 or 7 the Child really has outgrown all things that annoy, just at the time when as the charm of infancy begins to diminish, they would begin really to annoy—[*CN* III 3782]

The 'tender yet obedience-exacting & improvement-enforcing' parent he tried to be appears in another question to himself about how to instil honesty:

July 6, 1810.[1] I know few questions more delicate in Education than this: How shall we manage that ordinary but in its indefinite extent vicious assurance / if you will tell the truth, I will never be angry—I will never punish you—without bribing the mind, & inserting inward falsehood & Selfishness in order to produce a verbal veracity—& yet without expecting too much from Childhood. Perhaps, the

[1] Sara was 7, Derwent 10, and Hartley 14.

best way is—not to be angry, not to punish—but yet never to make such a promise, never to hold forth such a motive; but on the contrary, always to enforce the high feeling, that a noble mind ought almost to wish that the other should not escape its appropriate Blame & Penalty, in order that it may feel itself telling Truth for the sake of Truth. [*CN* III 3950]

His own struggles as parent-teacher, and teacher of many children with whom he came into easy, playful, often romping contact, come out in some reflections on the English alphabet.

Q[uer]y? Whether, in teaching Children to read, it would be worth the while to remove the obstacle of the naming of ⟨the⟩ Letters? Surely, an Obstacle it is—& such as must and does perplex a child, and offend too against the first great Law of Education, as far as possible to avoid all willkühr [*Willkuhr*], arbitrary will, dark and irrational—Ex. gr. Double U, Aitch, O, Ess, E = Whose? A Conjuror presenting a Plumb Cake and then turning it into an open-mouthed Wolf might impress more terror but not more sense of Unlikeness—or a bolder demand on the Child's Faith than to tell him that the Sound, Whose, is composed of the Sounds, Double U, aitch &c?—Bee a ell ell is Beaellel not Ball— . . .

He battles away with impossible solutions and finally concludes: 'On account of our lying Alphabet it would be better to teach to read in Latin or Greek'. [*CN* III 4324]

But, eager though he was for children to learn to read, his deepest concern was with moral education, and by moral education he meant something more than truth-telling in the sense of verbal veracity. Education must be gentle, truly an *educing* what is within.

His subtle insights into the minds of very young children are often uncanny and, like so many of his other perceptions, they anticipate future developments. About some of the later stages of education in schools and universities his foresight is portentous—and cold comfort to us to-day:

19 July 1826. The noblest feature in the character of Germany I find in the so general tendency of the young men in all but the lowest ranks. (N.b. and highest) to select for themselves some favorite study or object of pursuit, beside their *Brodt*-wissenschaft—their Bread-earner—and where circumstances allowed, to choose the latter with reference to the former. But this, I am told, is becoming less and less the fashion even in Germany; but in England it is the misery of our all-sucking all-whirling Money-Eddy—that in our universities those, who are not idle or mistaking Verses for Poetry and Poetry for the substitute instead of (as it should be) the corolla & fragrance of the austere and many Sciences, appreciate all knowlege as means to some finite and temporal end, the main value of which consists in its being itself a means to a ~~some~~ another finite & common end—Knowlege—Profession—Income—and consequently selecting their particular Profession in exclusive reference to the probability of their acquiring a good income &, perhaps ultimately a Fortune thereby, then set about getting in the easiest way exactly that sort and that quantity of knowlege, which will pass them in their examinations for the Profession, and which is requisite to or likely to forward their ~~professional~~ views of making money in ~~the~~ or by his Profession. . . . But this is the worst sort of Slavery: for herein true Freedom consists, that the outward is determined by the inward, as the alone self-determining Principle—what then must be the result, when in the vast majority of that class in which we are most entitled to expect the *conditions* of Freedom, and Freedom itself as manifested in the *Liberal* Arts and Sciences, all Freedom in stifled & overlaid from the very commencement of their career, as men—namely, in our Universities, Schools of Medicine, Law &c? [Folio N *f46*]

'Freedom is stifled', and Mammon confused with God, he thought, by lack of imagination, the best weapon against the old Adam in man:

> . . . in the imagination of man exist the seed of all moral and scientific improvement. . . . The imagination is the distinguishing characteristic of man as a progressive being; and I repeat that it ought to be carefully guided and strengthened as the indispensable means and instrument of continued amelioration and refinement. [Lecture of 3 March 1818]

In the conviction that 'the outward is determined by the inward as the alone self-determining Principle', Coleridge always stressed, as the absolute moral need and responsibility of any society, the preservation of its soul by providing for its children a continuing education in consciousness, the development of the self-conscious imagination not as part of the decor of the social stage but as essential to the main action. A continuously sensitive consciousness, growing and deepening as the individual grows and his society changes, is essential to moral freedom. The trouble with slavery to conventional, or heedlessly-acquired, or self-centred, or any other inadequately-conscious ends is that such slavery paralyses the universal principle of active growth. The trouble with the otherwise virtuous Southeys of the world, he thought, lay just there. Not only was the unity of personality violated by an unbridged gulf between doing and being, between performance and person, but this limitation in his very existence cut him off at the very point of relationship with others on which the continuity of society depends. Wordsworth, Coleridge found increasingly in later life (as the country folk in the Lakes also found), made himself unapproachable from a similar hard edge. Coleridge called it 'self-idolatry', 'self-ness', 'self-concentration', 'self-vorticity'; Wordsworth, he thought, had seriously damaged by it his own inner being, his relation to other persons, and his creativity.

. . . *In*firmities sunk under, the Conscious Soul mourning and disapproving, are less hindrances than *Anti*-firmities— such as *Self*-ness . . . and *separative*—instead of being, what it ought to be, at once *distinctive* and yet, at the same moment or rather, act, *conjunctive*, nay, *unificent*. [*CN* III 4243]

The self is under the constant necessity of 'combining with all things' as he put it. The ego must be huge, active, outgoing, so comprehensive as to become selfless.

—O there are Truths below the Surface in the subject of Sympathy, & how we *become* that which we understandly behold & hear, having, how much God perhaps only knows, created part even of the Form.—[*CN* II 2086]

So, we may 'become that which we understandly behold', we may create part 'even of the Form' of life with which we sufficiently sympathize. In Coleridge's philosophy, there is a very real sense in which the self-conscious imagination may become the instrument whereby losing we may re-create our selves.

He was fond of quoting Proverbs 29:18: 'Where there is no Vision, the People perish.' The essential for the individual human being and his society alike is the constantly creative vision. Fully recognizing human frailty, one must achieve the inner freedom to maintain and share that vision.

III

THE SELF AND THE NATURAL
AND SPIRITUAL WORLDS

ONE has only to try to describe one's own enjoyment of a landscape—hills and streams and rocks and skies—to know how difficult it is, short of poetry, to share anything of it. Coleridge in *Frost at Midnight* and *This Lime Tree Bower*, to take but two instances, has so exquisitely conveyed the relation of inner and outer worlds, that some of us can never see 'silent icicles, quietly shining to the quiet moon', or overhead, the shadow of one transparent leaf dappling another, without recalling, as an experience, those poems. In the notebooks, an inveterate analyser, he was trying to extend his knowledge of how the outer-inner communication works, and also to annotate and extend his pleasures in the natural world, whether in Somerset, Germany, the Lakes, Scotland, Malta, Sicily, or Italy. Towards the end of his life, in the Netherlands, he was still responding sharply enough to a landscape to feel impelled to write in his notebook a few lines of verse; they are like an artist's notes for a painting, the half dozen lines of this wet water colour:

Water and Windmills: Greenness, Islets Green,
Willows whose trunks beside the Shadows stood
Of their own higher half, and willowy Swamps,
Farm-houses that at anchor seemed & on the inland sky
The fly-transfixing Spires—
Water, wide water, greenness & green banks
And water seen   [N 40 *f27*]

Coleridge has strewn descriptions of larger and smaller aspects of nature liberally throughout his published works, but generally in the prose works they participate as illustration, or metaphor, in some chain of argument in which they play a secondary role. Yet the notebooks provide, in some of his finest memoranda, what a less wasteful writer would have worked up into essays. Take this from the winter of 1803–4 in the Lakes:

The waterfall at the head of the vale (the circular mountain walled vale) white, stedfast, silent from Distance / —the River belonging to it, smooth, full, silent—the Lake into which it empties also silent / yet the noise of waters every where / Something distant / something near, Tis far off, & yet every where / —and the pillar of smoke / the smooth winter fields—the *indistinct* Shadows in the Lake are all eloquent of Silence—[*CN* 1 1784]

It is impossible to convey the multitude of those quick, sensitive, minute or grand, quiet or boisterous, visual, aural or tactile enjoyments of nature, exuberant or painful, headlong or meticulous, that crop up to delight one, sometimes out of a morass of personal miseries, economics, metaphysics, politics, and religion in the notebooks. There appears to have been for Coleridge a very real and healthy physical release in the open spaces of fields and mountains, rivers and oceans. In the Lakes he ran, climbed, shouted, leaped from rock to rock in swirling torrents, dropped from ledge to ledge down the precipices of Scafell without any of the gear of ropes, cleated boots, maps, and carefully charted routes that climbers to-day find necessary. He was one of the first— some say the very first—of the fell-climbers for pleasure. He normally as a walker took the high road, up and

over, as I discovered in Sicily in trying to track him; not
for him the low road in the valley or by the shore.
Returning from Scotland on foot, in a desperate attempt
to shake his addiction, he wore out his shoes doing 263
miles, he said, in 8 days. These violent measures did not
cure the complaint, but they produced some splendid
observations of lakes and mountains, and of Edinburgh.
The Malta journey failed of a similar purpose, but the
Mediterranean excited him to write some rich memoranda.

To select but one noticeable element in his written
observations, his language for light and colours, so far as
I know, did not exist elsewhere in English writing in his
day; he was seeing the colours of French impressionism
a hundred years earlier. I am reminded, too, of certain
Englishmen who came to Canada about seventy years
or so ago and began painting our landscape in colours
that at first were considered shocking. Coleridge
noticed, for example, 'the dusky yellow richness of
Derwent water', 'raspberry and milk coloured crags',
the lake 'a mulberry-puce colour', 'the chocolate mist of
winter branches', violet-coloured beeches; not to forget
'that green light that lingers in the west' recorded
(contrary to those critics who have declared it impossible) many times in the notebooks. On the voyage to
Malta, off the coast of Portugal, basking in the sun,
watching the shadows of clouds 'many and large and
black on the broad Sides of the warm yellow green
mountains / like huge Phocae [seals] sunning themselves
on Sands', he continued in astonishment to revel in 'the
deepest purple Blue' of a promontory, and in abstract
patterns of the brightest and richest greens he had ever

seen, with equally light and bright violet purples—
against which he noted red caps on two fishermen, sails
ochre brown and 'Boys caps olive, less brown', 'Colours
remarkably soft & yet lively'. [*CN* II 2015] My point is,
his capacity for this sort of pleasure in colour. As in
other contexts he is uninhibited by the contemporary
conventions of observing. Here he is describing autumn
colours in the Lakes in October 1803:

O Thirlmere! let me somehow or other celebrate the
world in thy mirror. Conceive all possible varieties of Form,
Fields & Trees, and naked or ferny Crags—ravines behaired
with Birches—Cottages, smoking chimneys, dazzling *wet
places* of small-rock precipices—dazzling castle windows in
the reflection—all these within a divine outline in a mirror
of 3 miles of distinct vision! . . . All this in bright, lightest
yellow, yellow-green, green, crimson, and orange!—The
single Birch Trees hung like Tresses of Sea Weed—the Cliffs
like organ pipes! And when a little Breath of Air spread a
delicious Network over the Lake, all these colours seemed
then to float on, like reflections of the rising or setting
Sun.—[*CN* I 1607]

All this, spontaneous in the observing, was deliberate
and effortful in the recording.

What, inwardly, did his attention to nature mean?
Various things:

26th Septr Syracuse . . . I was standing gazing at the starry
Heaven, and said, I will go to bed the next star that shoots /
Observe this in counting fixed numbers previous to doing
any thing, &c &c &c and deduce from man's own unconscious acknowlegement man's *dependence* on some thing
out of him, on something more *apparently* & believedly subject
to regular & certain Laws than his own Will & Reason / It
is Saturday morning, 27 Septr 1805 / [*CN* II 2672]

It was to be anticipated that he would look outwards, then, for that stabilizer he had difficulty in finding within, as in Grasmere in 1809:

> O! Heaven! one thousandfold combinations of Images that pass hourly in this divine Vale, while I am dozing & muddling away my Thoughts & Eyes—O let me rouse myself—If I even begin mechanically, & only by aid of memory look round and call each thing by a name—describe it, as a trial of skill in words—it may bring back fragments of former Feeling—For we can live only by feeding abroad. [*CN* III 3420]

Everyone who has seen persons in deep depression or certain kinds of mental illness will recognize Coleridge's effort here to use nature for personal therapy. As a guilt-stricken traveller with a sense of running away from unfulfilled hopes and plans and thus avoiding his own continuity, he looked at himself contrasted with the fountains of Rome, waterfalls, a column of smoke even:

> The quiet circle in which Change and Permanence *co-exist*, not by combination or juxtaposition, but by an absolute annihilation of difference / column of smoke, the fountains before St Peter's, waterfalls / GOD!—Change without loss— change by a perpetual growth, that ‹once constitutes & annihilates change› the past, & the future included in the Present / oh! it is aweful. [*CN* II 2832]

In acute loneliness in the almost total absence of congenial society in war-time Malta in 1805, he said to himself in his notebook, 'You can walk no where without having whispers of Suicide, toys of desperation'. [*CN* II 2100] Nevertheless he 'roused' himself to feed abroad on many natural beauties. It was nearly May when he landed there, and he was at once struck by the trees, oranges and lemons with fruit and blossom together on the branches. He found the 'Pepper tree very beautiful' [*CN* II 2101], and many other fruits delighted him. Basic to therapy was the sheer pleasure:

2 April, 1805 The first yellow green leaves. Of the figures scattered all over the Tree, & yet thinly, & yet disclosing every branch & every grey twig resembled to a wonder a flight of large green Butterflies alighted on the leafless Tree / all shot through with Sunshine. [*CN* II 2518]

Then he added a correction. The new leaves were *not* 'all over the tree', 'no! only at the extremities of each twig'.

Coleridge was not a sloppy observer, and in scores of notes he enjoyed the effort involved in good close observation:

Pomegranate in beautiful scarlet Flower / under a Bridge over a dry Ditch saw the largest Prickly Pear / elk horns for Trunk, & then its leaves, but go & look & look / . Hard rain / [*CN* II 2102]

What the notebooks make clear is that part of the pleasure in studying the pomegranate trunk or the architecture of an intricate flower was, 'the sense of difficulty overcome', to use his own phrase for one of the pleasures from poetic composition.

... Arbour of a scented Butterfly-flower, but all conch-shaped, or cork-screw / the Standard [a] beautiful spiral, white stained with purple & the conformation of the Keel beautiful & curious beyond my power to describe; it ends in a compressed elastic cork-screw, which lies spire touching spire, but you can pull it out into a compleat screw; and this is continued, as it were finely spliced on to, & spun out into, the mast as we used to call it / which here seems rather to grow at the root of the Standard than on the Keel, and which splits into exquisitely subtle Threads. I should like to see Linnaeus on this Subject / . . . [*CN* II 2140]

Again, of the sea:

O said I as I looked on the blue, yellow, green, & purple green Sea, with all its hollows & swells, & cut-glass surfaces —O what an Ocean of lovely forms!—and I was vexed, teazed, that the sentence sounded like a play of Words. But it was not, the mind within me was struggling to express the marvellous distinctness & unconfounded personality, of each of the million millions of forms, & yet the undivided Unity in which they subsisted. [*CN* II 2344]

In this struggle to express the sense of 'unity in multeity' in nature we are on the edge of a very deep personal and religious problem, to which we shall return later. For the moment the wrestling is to translate a sensuous experience into words, an activity of the limitations of which, sometimes from the vastness of the subject, some-times from its interior depth, he was very conscious.[1]

The following three entries succeeded one another in Notebook 21, in December 1804 in Malta:

A brisk Gale, and on the spots of foam that peopled the *alive* Sea most interestingly combined with the numbers of white Sea Gulls; so that repeatedly it seemed, as if the foam-spots had taken Life and Wing & flown up / the white precisely same-color Birds rose up so close by the ever perishing white wave head, that the eye was unable to detect the illusion which the mind delighted indulging— [*CN* II 2345]

O that Sky, that soft blue mighty Arch, resting on the mountains or solid Sea-like plain / what an aweful adorable omneity in unity. . . . To the eye it is an inverted Goblet,

---

[1] *CN* I 1554; see above Lecture 1, pp. 9–10.

the inside of a sapphire Bason; = perfect beauty in shape and color; to the mind ⟨it is⟩ immensity, but even the eye ⟨feels as if it were to⟩ look *thro'* with dim sense of the non resistance / it is not exactly the feeling given to the organ by solid & limited things / the eye itself feels that the limitation is in its own power not in the Object, but pursue this in the manner of the Old Hamburgh Poet—[*CN* II 2346]

One['s eye] travels along with the Lines of a mountain— / I wanted, years ago, to make Wordsworth sensible of this— / how fine is Keswick Vale, would I repose? My Soul lies & is quiet, upon the broad level vale—would it act? it darts up into the mountain Tops like a Kite, & like a chamois goat runs along the Ridges—or like a Boy that makes a sport on the road of running along a wall, or narrow fence—[*CN* II 2347]

The response to a landscape and seascape was, as for most of us, in part kinetic:

. . . The Heavens lift up my soul, the sight of the Ocean seems to widen it. We feel the same Force at work, but the difference from Body & Mind both that we should feel in actual travelling horizontally or in direct ascent, that we feel in fancy—for what are our feelings of this kind but a motion imagined? . . . [*CN* II 2357]

The self in contact with natural beauty then, is able as he said, to 'issue forth' in search of some support, but it often recoils on itself. In Sicily, gazing at the mountainous Calabrian coast over the open sea he saw 'the Ships, the beautiful sparonaras, the fishing Boats, the white Sails of the Mediterranean / O even but 3 years ago how should I have *hoped* & schemed amid all this, but now I *hope* no more. O this *is* a sore affliction to be so utterly estranged from Hope / —'. [*CN* II 2705]

Again looking at those Mediterranean skies,

such *profound* Blue, *deep* as a deep river, and deep in color, &
those two depths so entirely *one*, as to give the meaning and
explanation of the two different significations of the epithet.
. . . Unconsciously I stretched forth my arms as to embrace
the Sky. . . . deep Sky is of all visual impressions the nearest
akin to a Feeling / it is more a Feeling than a Sight / or
rather it is the melting away and entire union of Feeling &
Sight / And did I not groan at my unworthiness, & be
miserable at my state of Health, its effects, and effect-
trebling Causes? O yes! . . . Have Mercy on me, O something *out* of me! For there is no *power*, (and if that *can* be,
less *strength*) in aught *within* me! Mercy! Mercy! Sat. Morn. 2
o'Clock. S.T.C. [*CN* II 2453]

(Owen Barfield objects to what he calls Coleridge's
lack of 'reticence'. I must point out here that by quoting
I am depriving Coleridge of the privacy of the notebook.)

Not only the grander aspects of nature but the smaller
creatures were often self-analogies, or objects of self-
identification. Elsewhere[1] I have tried to show his
empathy towards the caged bird in a London street, the
fly imprisoned in a child's hand, the convulsive gasps
for breath of a stranded fish, the poor heavy flyers among
the birds—towards any creatures held down by whatever weights and chains of frustrating circumstance.
They no doubt offered to his guilty self-awareness the
contrast that his own chains seemed to be self-forged.
Yet sometimes the natural analogies were salutary. The
sight of an external impersonal object could illuminate
something within, or answer some need—to the mind
endlessly searching for light and answers. On his return

[1] 'Coleridge and Restraint', *The University of Toronto Quarterly*,
XXXVIII (April 1969).

in some conflict of mind to Grasmere in 1808 he wrote:

Mournful and dim as the moon oval in wane within the dusky white vapor, scarce preserving its form, & skirted by black rain-clouds—Such was my Love during my days of Despondency—yet as the eye gazes on that dim moon thro' the thickening turbid white Cloud, troubled whiteness, so still my thought was always of the love—and as the Cloud was white amid the Black all around because the moon was behind it, so was despondency not despair because of the Love: yea by its very mournfulness preserved from Despair —for asking Pain is Life. [*CN* III 3371]

The consoling and important reflection is that in our emotion-dictated uncertainties we can take comfort from the panorama of a universe governed by change according to law. Certainly there was in 'those obscure feelings' a consciousness of a dynamic human relation to physical nature,—more than just that of an observer trying to describe it.

Important remark just suggests itself—13 Novr 1809—That it is by a negation and voluntary Act of *no*-thinking that we think of earth, air, water &c as dead—It is necessary for our limited powers of Consciousness that we should be brought to this negative state, & that [it] should pass into Custom— but likewise necessary that at times we should awake & step forward—& this is effected by Poetry & Religion / —. The Extenders of Consciousness—Sorrow, Sickness, Poetry, Religion—.—The truth is, we stop in the sense of Life just when we are not *forced* to go on—and then adopt a permission of our feelings for a precept of our Reason—[*CN* III 3632]

A person suffering from Coleridge's anxieties and nightly terrors needed that extension of consciousness into what he called 'the sense of Life', a sense of a larger order of

cause and effect, to fend off on the one hand private
Hells, and on the other the anti-intellectual chaos of
popular superstitions. Otherwise, he said,

No Sleep for Sleep to rest in—to the Superstitious who make
their very sleep *expensive* by fortune-tellers &c—Without rule
and without reason, they are as contingent, as if a man
should study to make a prophesy and by saying 10,000 things
may hit upon one true, which was therefore not *fore-known*
tho' it was *forespoken*: and they have no certainty, because
they have no natural Causality nor Proportion to these
effects which many times they are said to foresignify. [*CN*
III 3634]

There are other attacks on superstition, but for the
moment, one is to notice the confidence given by Nature's
'rule' and 'reason', to force ourselves 'to go on' extending our consciousness of our true context, our human
participation in the impersonal laws of natural Causality.

. . . The most pregnant historic Symbol on Earth is a Coral
Bank on a Stratum of Coal—or rather a quarry of veined
Marble on a Coal Stratum. The Peat Moor and the Coral
Bank, the Conjunctions copulative of animate and inanimate
Nature!—Lime fertilizing Peat, and thus mutually effectu-
ating each other's re-ascent into Life, the Peat into the nobler
Gramina, the almost animalized Wheat, the shelly Lime
thro' the Grasses into atmospheric red Life, and ending its
brief cycle in Man! . . .[1] [*CN* III 4432]

[1] This ties in with *The Theory of Life* (p. 86), 'In Man the centripetal
and individualizing tendency of all Nature is itself concentred and
individualized—he is a revelation of Nature! Henceforward, he is
referred to himself, delivered up to his own charge; and he who stands
the most on himself, and stands the firmest, is the truest, because the most
individual, Man. In social and political life this acme is interdependence;
in moral life it is independence; in intellectual life it is genius. Nor does
the form of polarity, which has accompanied the law of individuation up
its whole ascent, desert it here. As the height, so the depth. The intensities
must be at once opposite and equal. As the liberty, so must be the

He frequently noticed with something like triumph, the difficulties in defining the edges of the mineral, vegetable, and animal kingdoms,[1] as if here he saw evidence of process itself, growth, continuity with change, and change with continuity. In short, in looking at nature he saw the inside of the outside and the outside of the inside—he felt, at his best, a small but functional part of all that lives, grows, changes, and creates. Perhaps the importance—or one aspect of the great importance of 'hope' lay for Coleridge in this felt need of participation in vital processes. His insistence, too, on a 'dynamic' philosophy and on vitalist theories of life, had its roots here, as well as in his personal sense of *energy*; energy was to him a real *fact*, as well as a necessary principle of life. I think Coleridge's own sheer *energy*, of body and soul, in theory and practice, is deplorably underestimated. Certainly the notebooks make it visible.

We can see the intensity of the energetic work of extending consciousness, for instance while he looked out his window in Vallette, and into himself at the same time. Notice how he tried to leave the doors to 'the semi-demi-conscious' 'obscure feelings' open:

Saturday Night, April 14, 1805—In looking at objects of Nature while I am thinking, as at yonder moon dim-glimmering thro' the dewy window-pane, I seem rather to be seeking, as it were *asking*, a symbolical language for

---

reverence for law. As the independence, so must be the service and the submission to the Supreme Will! As the ideal genius and the originality, in the same proportion must be the resignation to the real world, the sympathy and the inter-communion with Nature. In the conciliating mid-point, or equator, does the Man live, and only by its equal presence in both its poles can that life be manifested!'

[1] E.g. *CN* III 3476, 4434.

something within me that already and forever exists, than observing any thing new. Even when that latter is the case, yet still I have always an obscure feeling as if that new phaenomenon were the dim Awaking of a forgotten or hidden Truth of my inner Nature / It is still interesting as a Word, a Symbol! It is Λογος, the Creator! <and the Evolver!> [*CN* ɪɪ 2546]

A Word, a Symbol, Logos, the Creator, Evolver. The newly observed phenomenon is intuitively recognized as a relationship, a mysterious truth of communication between the single mortal human being and the universal eternally creative principle under whatever name.[1] The last one, Evolver, is worth a moment's pause; Coleridge may have invented it. The *Oxford English Dictionary* cites his 1825 lecture 'On the Prometheus of Aeschylus' for its second occurrence, Thomas Taylor in the *Annual Review* for 1803 providing the first—but in so different a context as scarcely to be the same use. Certainly Taylor was not applying it to a cosmic principle.[2] Not too much should be read into this one word, *evolver*, however, for it could be simply a characteristically Coleridgean coinage from the Latin root, not necessarily resting on any broad concept. One may find in Coleridge both resistance to and advocacy of the evolutionary idea, which in one half-fantasied fragment he described as 'the potenziation of the ascending intensity of Life'.[3] While he opposed the crude pre-Darwinian biological evolutionism as he understood it, he said in the seventh of the

[1] The terms were enlarged upon with Platonic overtones in *CN* ɪɪ 2445.
[2] Coleridge however had read that issue of the *Annual Review*; see *CN* ɪɪ 1848 and n.
[3] MS Egerton 2800 *f155* in *Inquiring Spirit* §185.

Philosophical Lectures that he did not consider the notion of the evolution of human instincts 'at all extravagant'.

Wherever the truth lies in Coleridge's conflicting statements about evolution, there is no doubt that man was for him the apex of natural processes of the phenomenal world. At the same time, with these terms, Word, Symbol, Logos, Creator, and Evolver we are catapulted into the very centre of his religious interests.

In one of his late notebooks, kept in the last year of his life, he was struggling once more to explain the identity of pantheism and atheism, and that 'there is no consistent Medium, no abiding-place for the Mind, between Atheism, and the *Catholic* faith', by which he meant, mainly, between atheism and a trinitarian view of God. (The Trinity he held to be an inexplicable mystery, an Idea held on faith or not at all.) But as so often before, he tried to say what it is about Ideas that makes them inexplicable, essentially unutterable, certainly unverifiable, and yet known in experience. In N 52 he attempted a version of what he meant by the relation between what he so often called the great I AM in capital letters, and what after that may be called the little i am in lower case letters, the Logos and man, the infinite creativity and the finite creativity, the Creator and the human imagination.

N.B. One of the metaphysical puzzles or dreamings of my *Boyhood*—& which have never ceased off and on to revisit me [the question of why it is not possible to convey an Idea adequately, but only 'a rude *Image* of it'] . . . It is indifferent whether I consider the Idea as numerically one yet *Co*-present with ALL minds, tho' present *for* SOME only (viz. the awakened & directed thereto) or as a *Same, plurally* existing,

like a word distinctly heard by a thousand men, yet all
& entire for each. . . . The Idea cannot be conveyed; but
there are magic sounds & magic Combinations of Sounds
that have power either to awaken the Idea (i.e. to bring it
from its potential Being to actual Life) in the congenerous
minds / , or to raise, determine, and direct the mind to the
Beholding of the Idea. This Work is not the Idea, but the
ceremonial Rites by which I invoke it, or provoke to it. It
sounds like *mere* sound, differenced from noise only by
being articulated, to speak of a one and the same existing
plurally, yea in a boundless Multiple, without breach of
Identity, Unity, or Entireness— / And yet every Poppy in
the Garden is calculated to suggest the truth, to Him who
had beheld it as one Seed, traced its growth, and then con-
templated it at the fall of its petals in the matured Capsule
of ten thousand Seeds. The composite aggregates of the
Molecules or atoms of Carbon, Hydrogen, and Oxygen
which are the material conditions of the Visibility of the
Poppy, are many, & the visible Plant Images many; but the
Poppy remains one.—

   We are all successive Actualizations of the same infinite
Adam and the Individual Adam the commencing Poten-
tiality of which Point, the Initial Point. The Finite cannot
exist but with the Infinite—in every creature from a grain
of Sand to a Planet, from a Hydatid to a Man. [N 52 *ff14*^r–
15]

'The Finite cannot exist but with the Infinite.' This is the
abstract metaphysical form of the statement, and for
Coleridge to the end of his tough-minded life it was
necessary to make intellectual explorations and affir-
mations about the relation of finite and infinite creativity. From this relation he adduced his humility and
faith in a superior power. But in what order did
Coleridge arrive at faith and how resolve the doubts of
his precocious, radical, anti-clerical youth? What was

the process of his 'coming home', as one's old Methodistical forebears used to put it?

From the days of his earliest childish prayers ('Four Angels round me spread / Two at my foot and two at my head') to the final days when he asked to be left undisturbed, alone with his Maker as much as possible, Coleridge was a deeply religious person in the sense of living in awe of spiritual and moral powers. His youthful rebellion against the church of his fathers—and still more, of his brothers—was in the first instance a concomitant of radical politics and then a protest against the intellectual lethargy and social hypocrisy he found in the establishment. But neither Spinoza nor Unitarianism proved to be a solution of his personal problem. Positive elements in his developing religious views were, first of all the theological historicism of Lessing in particular, encountered with ardour in Germany in 1799, also Eichhorn's 'higher criticism' of the Bible as a set of documents. Then there was Kant's critical metaphysical boon of the distinction between verifiable and non-verifiable truth, which chalked out an area for faith which Coleridge transposed into something very like the one for poetry which he already knew in experience. He was quick to see the usefulness of that Kantian distinction between 'Reason' and Understanding (and to carry further than Kant the meaning of the 'Reason' and to make his own use of it to include imagination) in explaining the validity of what neither logic nor law-court evidence could prove. Then Malta made Coleridge a more convinced Protestant, and at the same time made him think in less English and more cosmopolitan terms. On 3 November 1810, a few days after the bitter break with Wordsworth, he wrote in his notebook a Trinitarian confession of faith.[1] From 1810 to 1816 the notebooks show every sort of despair; entries diminish in number, and abstruse research became more abstruse. In 1816 in Highgate he encountered something very like Christian love, and in 1817 he met Hyman Hurwitz, founder of a Hebrew Academy in Highgate, who revived his youthful interest in Hebrew. He began a systematic re-reading of the Old Testament, and read widely in Jewish history and in the New Testament. On Christmas Day 1827 he took the sacrament for the first time since his Cambridge days. To the end, he continued to harry from the field the Unitarians, text-sparring fundamentalists, and all miracle-mongers; and equally all those of the established clergy resistant to the larger concepts of philosophy and science. His disgust at ecclesiastical snobbery was, as it had ever been, scathing, and his capacity for discriminating among fanatics and extremists, separating the wheat from the chaff, was remarkable in its psychological discernment.

Such a brief run-down of events and opinions does but touch on the outworks of his religious faith, and I think it is true to suggest that points of doctrine were all his life of secondary importance to Coleridge. Yet they were important enough for him to say that he never found any one church (nor any political party) completely to satisfy him. But he developed a strong affection for the ritual of the Church of England.

His *Confessio Fidei* of November 1810 begins: 'I believe, that I am a Free Agent, inasmuch as, and so far as, I have a will [did opium produce the qualification?]

[1] *CN* III 4005.

which renders me justly responsible for my actions, omissive as well as commissive. Likewise that I possess Reason, or a Law of Right and Wrong, which uniting with my sense of moral responsibility constitutes the voice of Conscience.' [*CN* III 4005] Free agency for him parallels closely, or rather is a part of the mental initiative, that activity of mind that permits self-consciousness to man as to no other creature—a thesis central to Coleridge's whole position. It is a belief, not a verifiable fact, but for him a logical requisite for thinking at all. Self-conscious awareness of this free agency is Conscience. He wrote, referring (in 1803) to some personal incident:

I resisted the Impulse—Why? because I could not endure my after Consciousness. Hence derive the immense Importance to Virtue of increasing and *enlivening* the Consciousness & press upon your own mind & as far as in you lies, on others, the connection between Consciousness & Conscience / . . . [*CN* I 1763]

Ten years later:

God manifests himself to Man, as a Legislator, by the Law of Universal Reason, the *obedience* to which is not only perfect Freedom, but the only possible Freedom: the Law appealing to the Free Will, i.e. Reason with the consciousness of Will is Conscience. Where there is no Law, there must be Tyranny. . . . [*CN* III 3866]

Or, putting it in another way, 'the notion of God is essential to the human Mind, . . . it is called forth into distinct consciousness principally by the Conscience' [*CN* III 4005]. The existence of God, like the principle of a free will, is 'absolutely and necessarily insusceptible

of a scientific Demonstration'. The conscience then is a
form of self-consciousness in which the free spirit com-
municates with its creator, and a condition of a sense of
continuousness with God, a sense which we saw was for
Coleridge also the essence of human communication.
Communication was easy, as in prayer, when Faith was
fidelity to a moral order of freedom under the law.
Prayer for many and long periods in his life was fraught
with difficulties for Coleridge; he longed for it, as for
real communication at all levels. In the summer of 1808,
en route to Grasmere he wrote:

The *habit* of psychological Analysis makes additionally
difficult the act of true Prayer. Yet as being a good Gift of
God it may be employed as a guard against Self-delusion,
tho' used *creaturely* it is too often the means of Self-delusion.
But I am not speaking now of what my understanding may
suggest but of that which the *Fact* reveals to & for *me*—it does
make Prayer, the sole instrument of regeneration, very very
difficult. O those who speak of Prayer, of deep, inward,
sincere Prayer, as sweet and easy, if they have the Right to
speak thus, O how enviable is their Lot! [*CN* III 3355]

Part of his difficulty was the assigning of personality
to God—yet the language of monotheism inevitably
applies personal pronouns and the most exalted personal
attributes to God. Coleridge therefore coined a word to
take care of the difficulty, the 'Personeity' of Deity. It
means the *being*, the self-ness, the *Ich-heit*, of God, better
perhaps, the *essence*, the *ipseity*, of God. We communicate
with this divine entity, a higher order of existence. By
prayer we strive towards it—talking to ourselves and
beyond ourselves to a higher creativity that nevertheless
we co-operate with by the effort of will.

Another difficulty not only in prayer but in the whole belief in God was the sense of guilt, of sin, until, as he wrote in a note of 1809:

An idea has just occurred to me—it seems important. Is not *Sin*, or Guilt, the first thing that makes the idea of *a* God necessary, instead of το θειον—therefore is not the incarnation a beautiful consequence & revelation of the το θειον first revealing itself as ὁ Θεος?—The idea escapes from me as I write it; but purify the mind by humility & self consciousness wholly *retrospective*, & again try to retrace it. To see the Gospel in a new light again—& again read Spinoza—to think vices mere necessitated movements, relative only as stench or roughness, we *know* to be false—but take it in the Kantean idea, as the Anti-type of the moral Law—suppose it like Cohesion—as that simply causing coherence, so this essentially demanding *morality*—& what becomes of Sinners? I feel the Clouds—yet sure there is something here.—[*CN* III 3510]

The entry is typical of Coleridge struggling to work out a difficulty—in this case the difficulty of Original Sin—existentially the polar opposite of 'the Moral Law'. Opinions differ as to what he meant by it, but the numerous references to it in the later notebooks point overwhelmingly not only to a personal conviction of sin, but to a sense of radical imperfection in human nature. In an entry of December 1827, interesting for its imagery and its date just preceding his return to the acceptance of the Eucharist, he writes—

. . . the extreme peril of *Security* / we must *cling* like Infants, who are still in the arms or in the clutch of an Alien, tho' their arms are round their Mother's Neck. In a state of triumph and security the first Adam dreams, of *becoming* a God, and the secure Christian will too easily mistake God for himself.—That the spiritual Life in him is Christ (= God manifested in the Flesh) and not Himself, he can only continue to know by reminding himself of his *base*, his *Nature*, being the *Contrary* to God. [N 36 *ff8–8ᵛ*]

The concept of Original Sin he held no more verifiable than the concept of immortality but both were essential to his religious humility and faith—the one as a necessary preliminary to the acceptance of redemption through divine grace, the other, equally, to man's endurances, hopes, and struggles. The one was imperative to his dependence on God, the other to self respect and the on-going struggle to transcend the old Adam. He begged fervently, as late as 1830, in an entry addressed to God, to be preserved from

the deadly Hensbane of Self-contempt, the worst and most concentrated form of Selfishness! For it is a shrinking down into the mere Self, an abstraction from the redeeming God. It is well to know and feel what we *should* be without God, But to contemplate our Self as actually existing without God, is frightful morally, and a contradiction philosophically: for only by the divine influence can the Creaturely Ground be actualized.

O merciful Father! for Christ's sake enlighten my faith, enliven my Hope, enkindle my Love. [N 44 *ff44ᵛ–45*]

As I have said, points of doctrine were secondary to such spiritual yearning towards the simplest and most universal basics of religious faith. The subtleties of the orthodox concepts of the Incarnation and the Atonement were difficult for Coleridge; the first he was slow to formulate to his satisfaction, and the second was long repugnant to him. His attitude towards certain other Christian mysteries was exploratory of their meaning, tentative, not easily satisfied, but not closed. In 1810 for instance he regards the doctrine of Transubstantiation and the adoration of the Host 'a frantic superstition, but not Idolatry'.[1] Later—it would be after 1829 when Sara Coleridge the younger was within range of her father's conversation—his views on the Eucharist had moderated. She wrote about them to Aubrey de Vere:

... I think they were deep & spiritual, but in perfect harmony & analogy with his view of baptism & all his other ways of conceiving religious subjects—they were perfectly—I think, what Pusey would call rationalistic. He would subscribe to no form of words supposed to convey a religious truth, on a merely supposed external evidence, such as what is called the tradition of the Church. All doctrines of the Eucharist which connected a spiritual presence with the elements, apart from the soul of the receiver, were separated from his faith by an equally impassable chasm. He sometimes discussed the different forms and phases of this doctrine, as I might turn over pink, blue, or yellow garments, with no thought of wearing such but only of considering which will suit others best. Just in this spirit STC used to defend Transubstantiation & contend that it was a more convenient form of belief than our Anglo-Catholic theory of the real presence. . . . [*CN* III 3847n]

On one more general matter it is unthinkable not to say a few words—his revolutionary new way of reading the Bible. Here if ever, he felt, the self-conscious imagination must be at work. He had gone to school to Lessing and Eichhorn, but what he offered was a highly personal interpretation of a true as opposed to a superstitious use of the Scriptures. Professor Reardon, whose chapter on Coleridge is a most helpful and condensed

[1] *CN* III 3868.

presentation of Coleridge in the perspective of the history of religious thought in Britain, attributes to him 'a more intelligent grasp of the nature and implications of the biblical problem than was possessed by any other Englishman of his time.'[1]

On this point there are two remarks to be made here. One is that Coleridge's extraordinary grasp of the biblical materials is based on extensive studying, seen in the notebooks, detailed work of a kind and to an extent not usually credited to him. The day by day, verse by verse, chapter by chapter readings, queries as to the Hebrew originals, other versions, rabbinical commentaries, opinions of the early church fathers, was the earnest hard work not of a textual scholar but of a religious man scrupulously trying to discover the truth. Particularly the history of the Jews concerned him, as the background for understanding the subsequent Christian development. (His commentary on the Decalogue is a *tour de force* of historical imagination.[2]) The second remark is that the real strength of his commentary on the Bible lies in what he had learned as a poet, of the workings of the human imagination; he attacked the literalists for what he attacked everywhere in life, the dead letter interpretation that answered neither to sound intellectual nor to emotional needs. What he dubbed 'Text marshalled against text' he hated, not only as futile and obscurantist, but as a pandering to all the bad passions of self-assertive 'positiveness' as against the humility of the true sense of 'certainty'. Positiveness and certainty were two of his opposites. Such dead-hand

[1] Bernard M. G. Reardon *From Coleridge to Gore* (1971), p. 81.
[2] *CN* III 3293.

controversies utterly blocked the imaginative grasp of the body of scripture as a whole. What had such arguments to do with love, human or divine? How could such disputants comprehend the Bible as the documentary expression of man's historical struggle to know God, let alone see it at the same time as a symbol and a part of God's reaching out towards man? Coleridge as a literary critic was always a man of flesh and blood and never forgot that in discussing any book he was dealing with a creative act, an attempt at a reconciling unity. Every poem e.g. was a two-way creative process—in the one direction between the mind of the poet and the poem, in the other between the poem and the mind of the reader. So he sees the Bible as a two-way creative operation between God and man. Coleridge often appears close to the 'I-Thou' concept of Martin Buber. Texts cannot be isolated, nor the interpretation of single events, like miracles; the real religious concern with the God-man relationship is too big. What the searching imagination finds in the Bible (given the active Will) is a hope for itself as a potential part of the whole historical creative process. In other words it finds there the expression of God's discipline of love. 'Religion', he says, 'consists in Truth and Virtue, i.e. the permanent, the *forma efformans*, in the flux of Things without, of feelings & images within / —well therefore the Scripture speaks of the Spirit as praying to the Spirit—the Lord said to my Lord / &c—God is the Essence as well as Object of Religion.' [*CN* II 2550] The farther self-analysis took him, the more mysterious and aweful the creature and the creation became. The humility with which Coleridge put Truth and Virtue at the centre of his own constant

reaching for that Essence is poignantly expressed over
and over again in many private memoranda: 'Not what
I understand, but what I *am*, must save or crush me!'
[*CN* III 3354]

In closing, it seems to me that we have barely touched
on some of Coleridge's thoughts and feelings and insights
as he confided them to his notebooks. The important
omissions would make a very long list. There is, however, one general consideration I should like to raise as a
final question. Critics, historians of thought, even
philosophers, giving Coleridge the highest sorts of
praise, lament his lack of a system. But for that lack,
they say, he might have been the greatest thinker,
philosopher, teacher, moralist, etc., that England ever
produced. Yet, suppose he had hewn or hammered himself into a firm, sound, complete structure, would he not
have become his own contradiction? He did not even
believe in a closed system. He believed in growth, the
'free life', with a deep antipathy to 'the confining
form';[1] he had what he called a 'rooted aversion to the
Arbitrary';[2] systems and system-making do tend to
become at some point arbitrary. He preferred 'method'
to system, and it will be protested by some that he did
not achieve method either. But that depends on what
you mean by it.[3] He said somewhere that the shortest
path gives one the knowledge best, but the longer way
round makes one more knowing. The fragments he left
us in such quantities certainly necessitate the longer way
round. They tantalize us into wishing to understand

[1] 'On the Principles of Genial Criticism concerning the Fine Arts' in
Biographia Literaria, ed. J. Shawcross (1907) II, p. 235.
[2] *CL* VI 557.
[3] See the Essays on Method in *The Friend* (*CC*) I 448–524.

him, and then, willy-nilly, into facing the questions he raised. The trick he plays on us is the educator's trick, who says, 'What do *you* think?', i.e., 'Do it yourself'. Inquire of yourself—setting out from the grimmest realities of the Self, and Self-consciousness, so as not to end there.

The end is larger. For Coleridge in the final analysis, the end was love, human and divine. To achieve it, he shows us, the road must be found through all the byways of the Town of Mansoul, to whatever habitation of God each inquirer finds for himself.